The Insights Revolution

maru/matchbox

The Insights Revolution: Questioning Everything

Andrew Grenville

maru/matchbox

ISBN: 978-0-359-05890-7

https://www.marumatchbox.com

Contents

Introduction 1

Chapter 1 – A Time of Transformation...............................4

Chapter 2 – Stop Taking Orders and Start Taking Action 23

Chapter 3 - Stop Analyzing in Isolation and Start Thinking Outside the Survey...47

Chapter 4 – Stop Asking Why and Start Making Connections..........61

Chapter 5 – Stop Trying to Learn Everything at Once and Start Being Agile and Iterative...70

Chapter 6 – Stop Treating Respondents Like a Commodity and Start Treating Them Like People..77

Chapter 7 – Stop Conducting Abusive Surveys and Start Putting People First...88

Chapter 8 – Stop Asking Complicated Questions and Start Asking Questions People Can Answer 108

What's Next?..119

Acknowledgements 122

References 125

Introduction

"Anything that takes us out of our comfort zones for a while can act as a reminder that the past we are used to may not be our best future."
Charles Handy, author and professor

The insights industry is in trouble. It's not growing, despite an explosion of information, decreasing costs and an increase in the need for informed decision making. And it still does not have real influence in the boardroom.

It is too often focused on what happened, and not on where to go and what to do next. It is drowning in data while thirsting for wisdom. It focuses on methodology instead of decision making. Its methods are based on century-old approaches that ignore new understanding of how we think and act. And it is gathering its data from people it treats like chattel, which leads to the results being unreliable if not downright wrong.

It's time for an insights revolution.

Many of the things the industry does today need to stop. And there are a great number of things we need to start doing. That's what this book is about.

It is powered by interviews with over 30 thoughtful insights professionals, marketers and strategists from around the world. Their commitment to insights and their stories of successful transformation are inspiring, but their concerns about the future of the industry are palpable. In addition to the interviews, I draw on a wide-ranging body of literature, as well as original research on research.

My desire is that this book helps you think afresh about what we do today, and what we should do tomorrow. I hope it can help explain to stakeholders why the things we have done in the past will not work in the future. I want it to encourage the industry to treat the people we gather information from with respect, so that they continue to grace us with their feedback.

In the first chapter, we set the stage by looking at the changes that are to come, how we got to where we are, and what our future could look like. The imperative for the insights function to transform from being an order-taker to an integrated and agenda-setting part of the business is explored in chapter 2.

The value of looking beyond the myopia of surveys to the broader context of all information is covered in chapter 3. Chapter 4 explains how asking people "why?" is not just unhelpful, it is dangerously misleading. And chapter 5 speaks to the folly of the long survey and the value of an agile and iterative approach.

Citizens and consumers are the focus of the remaining chapters. The often tone-deaf way we try to connect with people is examined in chapter 6, and we consider ways we can develop a much more positive and sustainable relationship with them in chapter 7. Finally, we examine how the changing ways people communicate will require us to completely rethink the ways questions are asked.

When I started my career in 1987, I was a market researcher. I have also been called a pollster. A newspaper once called me an upholsterer, but I think that was a misunderstanding.

Today, I would identify as an insights professional. That's because the world is changing. Surveys were once the primary, if not sole, source of insights into what consumers and citizens thought, felt and did. Today, we are swimming in a sea of behavioral data, and we know that our emotions can often be better measured through observation and biometrics. The profession is no longer just about commissioning and executing surveys. It is about absorbing information of all types and translating it into action.

"Insights" is the transition point between data and a decision. The insight is not the end goal. The next step is what matters. The insight is what the market research/consumer insights/business intelligence/market analytics function currently delivers. We need to move past that to providing solutions to the question "What do we do next?"

Chapter 1 – A Time of Transformation

"If you dislike change, you're going to dislike irrelevance even more."
General Eric Ken Shinseki, United States Army, retired

The world of market research is at a tipping point. It can't continue as it is, and it is about to change dramatically. The critical question is will it evolve, or become extinct? Both are definite possibilities.

The old ways of conducting market research are increasingly ineffective, and a wide array of new information options is available.

For almost a century, survey research had a lock on insights. Want to know what people did? Do a survey. Wish to understand what people are thinking? Do a focus group to figure out what is going on, and then quantify it. There were few other reliable sources of specific information on people's choices. But the world has changed, drastically.

The speed at which decisions need to be made has also increased dramatically. "We'll have the results to you next quarter" just doesn't cut it anymore. Information must be managed dynamically. As Finn Raben, Director General of ESOMAR, told me: "We can no longer afford to be the grey mice that live in a cupboard and say, 'Ah, but you know, it took six months, and it is perfect research.' Too late, pal. The company's moved on."

The world is awash with data on exactly what people do, when they do it, and whom they do it with. This flood of information is reshaping how we learn, what we can know, and the insights we can generate. The challenge now is piecing together the puzzle.

Nobody really knows exactly how much data there is, and how much data is being generated, because the volume is growing so fast. It's commonly suggested that about 90% of all the data in the world today has been created in the past few years. But let's just agree on this: we are drowning in data and desperately need people to transform the data into insights that shape decision making.

This need to tame and focus data is why market research professionals have an incredible opportunity. They are well positioned to harness this surge of information. But are they ready? Are they willing to make the changes necessary to move away from simply "doing surveys" to generating insights? I know that if we don't evolve we will be left behind.

Is the end near?

In writing this book, I had the privilege of talking to dozens of researchers, strategists and marketers around the globe. There was overwhelming consensus that change is coming, and quickly. "I think it's going to be fascinating to see where things go, but I don't think it's going to continue the way it's going for another 10 years," said Shawn Henry of Camorra Research in New Zealand. Why? Because the traditional market research approach has lost its lock on knowledge.

"In the beginning we had almost a monopoly on insights," says Antony R. Barton, Director of Product Innovation and Marketing Insights at Intel, "and that put us in a very special position, because nobody else had access to data. We had to do this survey, or we had to do this discrete choice, or this set of focus groups, because nobody else could get the data. And then, all of a sudden, there is this explosion of data. There are lots of ways to get at insights. I think the industry has struggled with that. Who needs a survey that takes nine weeks to complete? Or who needs focus groups where I will get back to you in six weeks?"

Elizabeth Moore, Director of Research, Insights and Analytics at Telstra in Australia, is one who has seen a big change. "I think the market research industry is really at a pivotal point," she says. "Traditional models are being disrupted, and the way we buy insights is changing significantly. There's a whole range of questions that, in the past, we would have gone to a market research house to help us answer, but we're now actually using big data and analyzing our data."

Shawn Henry foresees the need for an "Armageddon," a "violent change, where somebody comes in and does something dramatically different that basically makes everybody else antiquated and wipes out a good majority of the existing research companies. I think there's going to have to be a major disruption," he says. "I just don't see the industry being bright enough to change on their own. It's that whole 'if I'm not forced to change I'm probably not going to, especially if people are paying me money.'"

He is not the only one who sees the potential for an entirely different model that disrupts the status quo. Patrick Comer, Founder and CEO of Lucid—itself a disruptor in the sample world—recently told a cautionary tale at SampleCon, a sample industry conference. "The real threat is outside this room," he said. "It has nothing to do with other companies that are not present here. It is things outside our industry."

"I am reminded of the story of the New York Stock Exchange. I don't know if you remember, but there were two exchanges: The New York and the American Stock Exchanges. They fought over every single public offering for 100 years. It was a brutal battle down on Wall Street, between these two big exchanges. Then the internet happened, and within 10 years, almost all their liquidity left to go to the electronic exchanges: NASDAQ, all the ECNs, and the rest. They [the New York and American Stock Exchanges] had to merge, and now they represent a minority of all exchange traffic in equities in the U.S."

"That was an external technology threat, not a 'did they add a new feature set, or win a new client, or take another company public.' That's a big lesson for us in the room. We can get caught up in the ins and outs of who is doing what in this room, and not on what is happening everywhere."

At that same conference, Mark Menig, COO at PureSpectrum, went so far as to ponder whether there will even be a need for people's opinions: "In 10 years' time, will the human respondent even be a component of our data collection process? Or will we simply move in a direction of AI, machine algorithms, machine learning, probabilistic exercises, and Monte Carlo scenarios, which not only eliminate the human respondent from the data, but give you more accurate and more realistic outcomes for the insights you generate."

While there is widespread agreement that the future will have multiple streams of data, most see an ongoing role for survey-based research. The question is, what kind of change is coming?

While there is an infinite number of possible futures for the world of market research, there are three scenarios that I think are instructive. The first is the example of dinosaurs: mass extinction, but with a thriving set of descendants that do not resemble the mighty T. Rex. Another is shoemakers: once the sole source of footwear, they have been displaced by mass production driven by a relatively small number of designers and engineers. The third analog is video: once produced by a select few, it is now available to everyone, and is consumed more than ever.

Dinosaurs today

Dinosaurs are one of our society's enduring fascinations—just ask any four-year-old. One reason they capture our imagination is that they are a powerful reminder that the world changes, sometimes in the blink of an eye. Dinosaurs grew to the size of jetliners and ruled the earth for more than 100 million years. Then everything changed.

It's generally assumed dinosaurs became extinct. But the chickadee chirping outside your window and the seagull trying to steal your potato chips at the beach are reminders that, while T. Rex no longer rules the earth, the descendants of pterodactyls are everywhere.

Pterodactyls had the wingspan of an F-16 jet fighter. They were powerful, and terrifying. But they are long gone. So why did the dinosaurs that evolved into birds survive? Research suggests it was because they were smaller and nimbler.

What can we learn from dinosaurs? The nimble survive. And when behemoths fall, they fall hard.

This scenario suggests the demise of the market research industry as we know it. Large suppliers: gone. Big market research departments: so transformed as to be unrecognizable. But the insights function soars on, just in a radically different form.

The cobbler's children

For most of human history, shoes were made by hand. Skilled workers practiced their craft to create individually crafted shoes—all very similar, but each one slightly different. The process was repetitive, but custom. Just like surveys today.

Then came the Napoleonic Wars, and the Industrial Revolution. The need for huge numbers of boots for the soldiers of the British Army was the impetus for an engineer named Marc Brunel to devise a system for automating shoemaking. Sir Richard Phillips visited Brunel's factory and was greatly impressed by the speed and precision with which the boots were made. He also noted how the process eliminated the need for skilled labor and greatly reduced the cost.

In 1817, in *Morning's Walk from London to Kew*, Phillips wrote, "In another building I was shown his manufactory of shoes, which, like the other, is full of ingenuity, and, in regard to subdivision of labour, brings this fabric on a level with the oft-admired manufactory of pins. Every step in it is effected by the most elegant and precise machinery;

while, as each operation is performed by one hand, so each shoe passes through twenty-five hands, who complete from the hide, as supplied by the currier, a hundred pairs of strong and well-finished shoes per day. All the details are performed by the ingenious application of the mechanic powers; and all the parts are characterised by precision, uniformity, and accuracy. As each man performs but one step in the process, which implies no knowledge of what is done by those who go before or follow him, so the persons employed are not shoemakers, but wounded soldiers, who are able to learn their respective duties in a few hours. The contract at which these shoes are delivered to Government is 6s. 6d. per pair, being at least 2s. less than what was paid previously for an unequal and cobbled article."

Under this model, the shoe market was revolutionized. Once a precious and singular possession, shoes are now designed by a handful of people, manufactured with little manual labor and sold for anything from a pittance to a pretty penny—depending upon the company's ability to add value.

How many shoes do you have? I would wager it is many more than your great, great, great grandparents had at the dawn of the 19th century. And while each shoe is manufactured in the multi-thousands, it is rare to find someone wearing the exact same shoes as you.

In this scenario, survey research enjoys a much larger market than it does today, and is automated. This enables variety and scale. There would be just a handful of researchers designing studies, but there would be many more jobs for people whose role it is to sell the results by making them attractive and applicable.

Video everywhere

It is hard to imagine that not long ago video was rare and very expensive to produce. It is estimated that within the next few years, 80% of all internet traffic will be streaming video. As I take the subway to work, it seems half the people are gazing at their phones watching some form of video. The interesting thing is that most of them are watching completely different content. It is produced in great volume, but also in great variety. It wasn't always this way.

I've been producing video, on and off, since high school. Back then, the only way I could get access to a video camera was to sweet-talk my art teacher into kindly asking the school's audio-visual technician if I could use the one camera the school had. The picture was grainy, the camera needed a lot of light, and it was tethered to a very large, non-portable recorder. And there were no editing facilities, so everything needed to be shot in sequence.

After high school, I joined a local artists' association, where they had a couple of video cameras, including one that was "portable"—if you consider an enormous shoulder-mounted camera and a 20-pound recorder portable. That gear was worth about $50,000 in today's money.

To get access to editing equipment, I had to either talk the university into letting me use the film school's very rudimentary two-machine set-up, or I had to produce material for the local cable station—which had a very simple analog mixer.

Today I carry in my pocket a video camera (some call it a phone) that is vastly superior to the artists' association's camera. And I can edit the results on my laptop with infinite flexibility. With so much video being produced, there has been an immense increase in the number of people who make their living producing an incredible diversity of content. Business and personal use of video is up dramatically.

In this scenario, market research becomes quick and easy to execute, and is much more widely used. But it remains a craft—the skill of the maker determines how valuable the content is.

The future is in our hands

It's impossible to know which scenario will play out. It is quite probable that some combination of all these scenarios will transpire. But one thing these scenarios have in common is a radical change, creating new winners and losers. This change is not likely to be a single event. It is likely to be an ongoing process of continual, rapid evolution.

Disney CEO Bob Iger wrote in *The Economist* about the transforming world of media. His words are equally applicable to the domain of insights: "We once used the term 'disruption' to describe all of this [sweeping change], but the word now seems like a quaint relic of a bygone era, implying a paradigm shift with a beginning and an end, a before and after. What we are experiencing now is a state of perpetual permutation." To understand how we need to continually change and adapt, it is important to think about how we got here.

We have processes, customs, and assumptions that history and tradition have bequeathed us. Some of these will be enduring qualities. And some will be anchors that could snare us and tether us in place just as the flood waters of change rise and drown us.

Let's look at the forces that have shaped the insights industry today, so that we can be ready for tomorrow.

The roots of market research

Surveys are so common ("On a scale of 0 to 10, how likely are you to recommend this book to a friend or a colleague?") that it is hard to imagine a time when they did not exist. But, indeed, what we call the market research industry is less than 100 years old—a mere blip in humanity's journey.

The direct antecedent of today's survey research industry started in the 1920s, but it came to prominence when George Gallup used sampling theory to gather results that enabled him to correctly predict the 1936 presidential election. At the same time, *Literary Digest*'s "straw poll" got the election results spectacularly wrong (more on that in chapter 6). This made the importance of good sampling crystal clear.

This triumph of "scientific" surveying traces back to three earlier developments: social research, psychometrics, and sampling theory.

Social research

Social research efforts emerged at the end of the 19th century. Famous early studies included Charles Booth's *Life and Labour of the People in London*—an in-depth look at the social conditions of the poor—and the *Hull House Maps and Papers of 1895*—a study of poverty in a portion of Chicago. These studies were not the kind of very narrow survey research we do today. They were more sprawling, omnivorous investigations—the kind we talk more about in Chapter 3.

"In Booth's time, the survey did not specify or imply specific modes or instruments of data gathering, such as interviews or questionnaires," writes Jean Converse in her excellent *Survey Research in the United States: Roots and Emergence 1890-1960*. "Indeed, as we have seen, the early social surveys used a melange of techniques—the more the better—to gather data: questionnaire, interview, letter, direct observation, participant observation, systematic counts of observed behaviors, physical examination and measurement of houses and human beings; family budgets of income and expenditure; and aggregate data on population, migration, births and deaths, health and disease, wages, and prices."

Booth's investigation inspired people because it revealed that which was ill-understood and painted a compelling and unsettling portrait of life in London. It did what research does best: expose the richness of reality.

Psychometrics and the measurement of attitudes

Booth's enthusiastic investigations were deep and rich, but they did not embrace the kind of formal quantitative methods of asking questions that are so commonplace today. More focused and quantitative surveys sprang largely from the development of psychological testing.

The first modern intelligence test was developed in 1904 by Alfred Binet and Theodore Simon. They were commissioned by the French

Ministry of Education to devise a test that would distinguish "mentally retarded" children from normally intelligent but lazy children. At the same time, others were developing psychological measures that aimed at providing a precise account of belief and behavior.

James McKeen Cattell, in his classic 1895 paper *Mental Tests and Measurements,* set the groundwork when he wrote, "Psychology cannot attain the certainty and exactness of the physical sciences, unless it rests on a foundation of experiment and measurement. A step in this direction could be made by applying a series of mental tests and measurements to a large number of individuals."

The study of attitudes and their measurement began to flourish in academic social psychology in the early 1920s. If we want to reflect on why we use the measures we do, it is crucial to understand that the psychologists who developed these measures worked primarily with their university students. Their interest was in developing academic measures of complex issues, and students were ideal.

According to Converse, "First, one needed people with some talent for attitudes—literate, comprehending, articulate, and self-conscious to some extent about their intellectual, political, and moral positions; people, in sum, who were trained in having attitudes . . . . Students also did not pose problems of academic translation—that is, they did not require the simplified wordings, less abstract ideas, and concerns and situations that were closer to common experiences among the broad public. Second, one needed people with the time and tolerance, and students could be—gently—imposed upon."

Does that sound like the person doing your survey, who was attracted by an ad offering to "put cash back into your wallet"? Do they have "time and tolerance"?

This has important implications for us, because many of the types of complex scales and measures we use trace back to the work of these psychologists. We inherited a template for how to ask questions that has very little to do with the world we live in today. We discuss the impact of that, and the need for change, in Chapter 8.

Sampling theory

There are not too many people who get excited about sampling. But representative and reliable sample is the backbone of survey research. Without it, the whole enterprise will fail. Bad sample means incorrect results, leading to wrong decisions. With bad sample, we imperil the reputation of the entire industry.

The notion of sampling is also relatively young. Anders N. Kiaer, the director of the Norwegian Bureau of Statistics, first proposed sampling at a meeting of the International Statistical Institute (ISI) in 1895. Many people thought that the idea of not using a census to measure the population was heretical. Kiaer was able to show that his methods, as he refined them, produced results that matched the census. But it was 1906 before an Englishman named Sir Arthur L. Bowley introduced the idea of probability theory in sampling at an ISI conference. He was the first to suggest the error in a sample could be measured. And he was so bold as to suggest samples could replace a census.

Polish statistician Jerzy Neyman ushered in the modern era of sampling with his 1934 publication *On the Two Different Aspects of the Representative Method: The Method of Stratified Sampling and the Method of Purposive Selection.* "Sampling statisticians view the 1930–1940 period as the practical start of their profession," writes Robert Groves, former Director of the U.S. Census Bureau. "Neyman's article in 1934 convincingly presented evidence that probability sampling offered bias-free estimates and measurable sampling errors. The early founders of that field in the United States told of the excitement of young statisticians in Ames, Iowa, and Washington, DC, studying his paper, bringing Neyman over to visit, and teaching each other its implications. There is even an oft-repeated story of their using the meeting table in the U.S. Secretary of Agriculture's office (then a department that was a hotbed of survey development) to meet after the workday to discuss new developments." The work of Neyman and the U.S. government researchers also shaped the efforts of market research pioneers Gallup, Starch and Roper.

The new scientific approach to sampling gave survey research the representativeness and reliability it needed to have widespread application. Now researchers knew they could ask a properly selected subset of the population a question and get the same answer twice. Without those advances, the business of market research would not exist today.

Good thing Neyman is not alive to see how most sampling is done these days. He would be appalled. Sadly, as an industry, we have largely abandoned what was learned about representative samples. This has been driven by three powerful forces: a decline in trust, a change in how people communicate and—most importantly—an insatiable desire to reduce the cost of doing research.

Sample is research's Achilles' heel

What started as a slow, downward slide in sample quality is now a race to the bottom, at blistering speed. Unless we quickly course-correct, it is sure to end in a terrible, and potentially fatal, crash.

How did we get from Neyman's brilliant advances to sampling so sloppy it provides misleading results?

When George Gallup sent out his interviewers door to door, research was a novelty. Public trust was high and ordinary people were flattered to have someone ask their opinion. According to Groves, "With response rates often over 90 percent, there was more concern with contact rates than refusal rates." But people stopped wanting to give up their time, and they became less comfortable inviting strangers into their homes. Response rates declined, and so did representativeness. Besides, door-to-door surveying was slow and expensive.

At the same time face-to-face surveys were becoming less popular, telephones became so commonplace that almost everyone had one. Researchers started using telephone surveys, even though they did not yield a fully representative sample because not everyone had a telephone. But their cost and convenience, and the speed with which you could do telephone surveys, were very seductive. And the method was still yielding good results and response rates were great—for a while. Then people stopped answering their phones, and then they stopped having landlines. Besides, everyone was using these newfangled computers, and this thing called the World Wide Web.

So, research followed the people online, for the most part. Researchers were not too troubled by the fact that not everyone had or used a computer—because they had gotten used to a lack of full representation with telephone sampling. Then the industry came up with new and clever ways to attract people to complete surveys. And the quality of that sampling (and sample sources) became wildly variable. We cover that in Chapter 6.

While most research migrated online, some organizations stayed with the telephone. Some, for cost reasons, continued to use interactive voice response (IVR). That's the famous "Press one if your answer is 'yes.' Press 2 if your answer is 'no.'" IVR has a very, very low response rate. Its representativeness and reliability are, therefore, highly questionable. However, because it is automated, it is very inexpensive to call tens of thousands of numbers—even if almost all of them ignore the call, or hang up.

The use of IVR is the source of an important cautionary tale about how bad sample can very publicly destroy the reputation of research and undermine our industry.

Conflicting results, insults and lawsuits

Calgary, Alberta, Canada is a beautiful city of just over 1.2 million people. It is picturesquely situated at the confluence of two rivers in the foothills of the majestic Rockies. It is also a place where polling went horribly awry, in a very public way.

The incumbent mayor of Calgary, Naheed Nenshi, was running for a third term in late 2017. Mainstreet Research, headed by Quito Maggi, was doing polling for Postmedia, a company that owns two prominent newspapers: the *Calgary Sun* and the *Calgary Herald*. Mainstreet and Postmedia released three polls in the weeks before the election, predicting Mayor Nenshi would lose to a relatively unknown challenger named Bill Smith. These results were at odds with other companies' surveys—which were only released later—as well as the mayor's personal polling.

Local political science professors expressed skepticism, and the Twittersphere blew up with statements like: "Would never trust this poll . . . . it's Postmedia propaganda" and "Cons[ervatives] just trying to swing an election with rigged poles [sic]. . . . we are not impressed."

When a poll was publicly released that contradicted their numbers, Mainstreet's Quito Maggi tweeted, "If polling were poker, this is the part where I would go all in; I would bet $10 million we're closer than that pseudo poll today."

When political scientist Duane Bratt tweeted, "Asking Canadians just released a poll on mayor's race that is pretty much the opposite of previously released polls by Mainstreet," Maggi fired back with "Your credibility is getting stretched the more you comment, let's just see in 5 days."

When the mayor's pollster Brian Singh publicly expressed his doubts, Mainstreet slapped him with a "cease and desist" letter threatening legal action for making libelous statements. The letter said that if the mayor's pollster continued to make "accusations or refuse[d] to retract [his] previous statements publicly," Mainstreet would "be forced to take legal recourse for the damages inflicted."

Mainstreet executive vice-president David Valentin also came out swinging, suggesting commentators were biased. "Certainly I've seen a lot of behaviour from political scientists that I would say is quite shocking in this election campaign, and some of it, quite frankly, is quite appalling," he told 660 News. Valentin also said that the company planned on "singling people out" for "what exactly it is they said and did" about the poll results. "I think anyone who comments to the media should expect that their comments are going to receive scrutiny after the fact," he said. "I think that's fair."

The Friday before the election, Valentin tweeted, "Some people are going to have a very bad Monday, but not me."

Mainstreet predicted an 11-point lead for Smith. In the end, Naheed Nenshi was re-elected with an 8-point lead over his top competitor. Whoops.

We all get to share in the hangover

On the Mainstreet website the next day Maggi wrote, "On Monday night, I watched with utter shock and embarrassment as results came in for municipal elections across Alberta and our final prediction in the Calgary municipal election was completely and totally wrong. Our final tally showed an 11-point win for challenger Bill Smith over incumbent Naheed Nenshi. The result was a 7-point win for Nenshi. Our final poll had underestimated the incumbent's vote by 12% and overestimated the challenger by 8% for a total deviation of over 20%."

Maggi admitted to CBC News that the second poll his company did, which had Smith ahead by 17 points, was based on a "wonky sample." "We knew that it wasn't a great sample, but it's the sample we get," he said.

Pollster Marc Henry of ThinkHQ Public Affairs, who conducted internal polling during the race, said his research showed that Nenshi had started with a 20-point lead among decided voters, and that the gap narrowed during a contest that got nasty. If that's the case, then Mainstreet could have been off by as much as 37% in the earlier stages of the race.

"We didn't put this number out there to be malicious, or interfere with democracy, or anything like what we've been accused of," Maggi told Global News. Mainstreet conducted a full investigation and promised to tweak their methodology.

Saskatchewan party leadership race

A few months later, Mainstreet did polling in neighboring Saskatchewan. There, the very popular Saskatchewan Party was electing a new leader to replace Brad Wall who, for many years, was the most favored premier in Canada.

Mainstreet released numbers a few days before that election. Global News reported Ken "Cheveldayoff has 46.2 per cent support among decided and leaning Saskatchewan Party voters, with Scott Moe the second choice at 21.5 per cent. They are followed by Alanna Koch (19.5 per cent), Gordon Wyant (9.7 per cent) and Tina Beaudry-Mellor (3.1 per cent)."

In the end, Scott Moe received 54% of the vote, and Cheveldayoff came third. Whoops.

The impact on public perception

Reg Downs is Senior Advisor to the Premier of Saskatchewan. He has also handled his party's polling file for all of its provincial election campaigns. These kinds of bad polls cause him problems because they influence public opinion. We spoke after the leadership campaign. "The problem is," he said, "media outlets do publish these things. People do tend to read them. I don't know to what extent they influence people, but I think they create an impression this party is winning, or this party is losing, and we have seen some terribly inaccurate stuff recently."

This puts Reg and the Party in a difficult position. "They put out some really inaccurate polls in Saskatchewan here," said Downs, "and then you're questioning their accuracy and their methodology. When you do that as a political party, it's difficult because you can come across as whiney. 'Oh, you are just saying that because you are losing.' No, we are saying that because they're inaccurate and they have a history of being inaccurate. So you are always having this discussion: Do we just ignore it? Do we let it go? Do you try to counter it in some way?"

He also noted poor-quality polls undermine the reputation of research. "A few examples of bad polls can make people question the entire industry," he said. "Even when you have what we consider to be an accurate pollster, people are sort of skeptical of the whole industry."

I use these examples not to pick on IVR, because there are many other terrible ways to sample too, but because they dramatically demonstrate how bad methodology can bring the industry into public disrepute. In recent years, more poor-quality polls (combined with an over-enthusiastic media) have caused many to question the validity of survey research.

Following the erroneous predictions leading up to the election of Donald Trump in 2016, the *New York Times* reported, "It was a rough night for number crunchers. And for the faith that people in every field — business, politics, sports and academia — have increasingly placed in the power of data."

Some very public polling misses in the U.K. provoked the House of Lords Committee on Political Polling and Digital Media to commission a report to consider the "effects of political polling and digital media on politics." In its report, the committee stated, "Our central concern was that, if it is becoming less likely that polls can provide accurate estimates of the likely election outcomes, then there is a significant risk that future elections will be affected by misleading information, potentially distorting the democratic process."

The report went on to say that the available data on longer-term polling performance trends suggest that "it would not be correct to say that we are witnessing a decline in the accuracy of polling" but that "although polling performance has not worsened in a statistically significant way, there is little doubt that confidence in polling has been shaken."

This skepticism has implications far beyond political polling. CEOs, marketers and other stakeholders in the industry follow the news too. And so do the public we ask to answer our surveys. After the Calgary debacle, Canadian industry group Marketing Research Intelligence Association launched their own investigation. Their CEO said, "We don't want the Canadian public to perceive that polling is a wasted exercise. Because it isn't, it is the voice of the people, but it has to be performed properly and it has to be reported properly."

Amen.

Moving forward, conscious of our past

Jesse Ventura, professional wrestler, actor, author and former Governor of Minnesota, gave us his version of an oft-recycled pearl of wisdom: "Learn from history or you're doomed to repeat it." In a time of evolution, repeating history is good, if what you are doing works. But repeating a dysfunctional approach is a sure road to extinction.

When we look back at our heritage, we can identify some ways in which we have moved away from our roots—much to our detriment. In other ways we have clung to the old ways—retaining methods that grind against the reality of today. We need to be aware of our heritage and think about whether it is helpful or hurtful.

The omnivorous approach of Charles Booth was very fruitful. He collected all sorts of information—including surveys. But it was his synthesis of all those sources that made his endeavors so impactful. We have too often been seduced by the easy answer of the survey. Context is critical. We should embrace many sources of information and let them all shape our perspective. We must return to our heritage.

Psychometricians were the kings of precision when survey research was a fledgling, attempting its first flights. But their influence imprinted on us too deeply. Methods that focused on precision in measuring the attitudes of 20th century university students in a laboratory are unhelpful when it comes to asking 21st century people on their mobile phone what they think about a new package of bacon. We need to rethink our assumptions about what's a good question.

The early raging debates about the validity of thoughtful approaches to sampling have been tossed aside for savings in cost and an increase in speed. This is insanity. It undermines the very premise of providing information that is true. Without truth, there is no point to an insights industry. Let's remember how good sampling gave wings to our fledgling endeavor.

We need to change.

Change is good

In the following chapters, we look at some of our current practices and how they might benefit from change. Change is not a bad thing; it is healthy, even though it is often hard.

Let's leave the last words in this chapter to Robert Groves, of the U.S. Census Bureau: "Survey research is not dying; it is changing. The self-report sample survey provides insights into the thoughts, aspirations, and behaviors of large populations in ways that data tracking naturally occurring behaviors are unlikely ever to capture. The survey method has strengths and deficits that are reflections of the society that it measures; … [it] is governed by norms that can and do change. Survey research has always and must always adapt to those changes."

Chapter 2 – Stop Taking Orders and Start Taking Action

The insights leaders of the future take action, not orders. They don't follow an agenda, they set it. They don't deliver data, they provide solutions to business problems. They lead from the core, rather than follow from the periphery. They are not part of a cost center, they generate income. That's the future.

The insights function is changing, rapidly. In the future, insights must act across the organization, not just as a servant of marketing. Simply being good at primary research will not be enough. It will be essential to be able to synthesize diverse streams of information to guide the business.

This chapter is built on interviews with insights professionals, marketers and strategists. What emerged from these discussions is a clear and exciting picture of where the insights function is headed. For many organizations, this transformation is underway. Some groups are further along than others, but everyone is clear on the need for change.

The old market research department is dead. A new insights function is being born.

As with any birth, there will be pain and joy, and no way of ever going back. There is only one direction: forward. This transformation must happen fast because the speed of business is increasing. Insights can either keep up or be replaced by some other timely source of information.

Before we look at the changes that must come, we need to understand how we got to where we are today. Then we can plot a new path forward.

Roots in reactive measurement

When research departments were first being set up, in the 1910s and 1920s, their role was primarily as an adjunct to marketing and advertising. According to *Survey Research in the United States*, "The earliest consumer research focused on consumers' reactions to products and advertising, especially advertising in magazines, newspapers, billboards, and direct mail. Leading publishing houses undertook research to demonstrate to their potential advertisers who and where their readership was and what products these readers would be likely to buy."

The focus was on measurement and providing data that would help support the buying and selling of advertising. Research was, notably, not focused on generating insights to drive innovation or improve the customer experience.

As Michael Greco, EVP Programming & Research at media giant Discovery Channel, told me, "Research in the past was a place for people to hide. It could be like a real backroom operation. It was the old, slip the numbers under the marketer's door, run the overnights, and 'here is what the estimates are.' That was what the bulk of research was doing."

According to London-based consultant Mike Stevens, "A lot of what we've been calling insight for years has just been measurement. It's been gathering data and reporting it back. There are a lot of people who are non-specialists in client research functions who are effectively project managers, who just pass a brief from a stakeholder to an agency; they manage the agency and communicate back to the internal stakeholder, do all of the admin and the budgeting, but don't really add much value strategically."

This kind of passive order taking can also lead to disengagement and an "I ticked the box" mentality. Pamela Mittoo, Manager, CCNA Product Guidance Global Research & Development at Coca-Cola Innovation, says of people in this mode, "They don't have any horse in that race. They don't care about the methodology that they choose. 'I'm just giving you what you asked for; if it fails, well, that's on you, but I know that I called the agency, and the agency did it right.'"

This approach gives research a bad name and utterly fails to realize the potential of an insights function. "There's just no way that we can sustain this slightly bookish, fence-sitting reporting of feedback data. We have to be much more front foot about it," Stevens says.

This "tick the box" mentality, coupled with territorialism and a study-driven pace, drives marketers mad—as it should. Pina Sciarra, who has held senior marketing and sales roles at packaged goods companies and is currently Managing Director at PwC Consulting, hates this model. She wonders why insights is even a separate function. "I feel like there shouldn't even be an insights group," she says. "I think everyone's brain should be wired—marketers, business people—on how to take that data and then have the agility to go do something with it."

She feels access to information should be seamless, and not be "The report is coming out in two months." She yearns for "Insight. Action. How does that information help your customer, and what is it doing to help drive revenue?" She decries the fact that "we are limited by: 'Well, that's not my department. I don't have that title.' Insights are insights. Shouldn't everyone be able to have access to that, and do something with it?"

Her plea is: "Why don't we get in the same room and build something that is more integrated?"

Excellent question.

From order taker to agenda setter

The order-giving and order-taking paradigm is self-defeating. It typically involves people who know a little, misdirecting the people who are the experts. And it requires investments of time and energy to get to the underlying issue—time that could be better spent solving the problem, rather than uncovering it.

In the order taker model, the stakeholder—typically marketing—comes and asks for some focus groups, or a concept test, or a usage and attitudes study. They may check a process box and say, "yes, we researched it. Here's the number to justify what we want to do." Or they may be too close to the problem and not seeing it in a broader context. Or they may be unaware of what information exists already.

In a worst-case scenario, the marketers have spent a little time in research, so they think they know exactly what they want. A little knowledge is a dangerous thing.

Maggie Kishibe, Brands Insights Lead at Twitter, explains, "The people who think they understand research think it's an easy task. But they're not doing a good job of it. They are the ones who will come to us and say, 'I need to measure X, Y, and Z in a study, and here you go: just go execute.'"

I asked her about dealing with people with no knowledge of research. She said, "They actually are better at coming to us to say, 'Here's the situation: I'm told I need to get data. I need your help.' And then, it's an open book. They're a lot easier to deal with because they already go to that step automatically. They don't try to prescribe what the question is."

When stakeholders come to the insights professional thinking they know what they want, the researcher's challenge becomes uncovering the root of the business problem. Kristopher Sauriol is Senior Director, Global Research and Insights at Visa. He says, "often what happens is someone will come to me, and they will say, 'I need a number because we are going in front of the CMO, and I need a number to prove why we should do X or Y.' My first response is then to say, 'Okay, hold on a second. What are we really trying to solve for? I don't know that it's necessarily a number that you need' and walk it back. Because, if you start from that point, you force yourself to end up there."

Mittoo takes requests with a grain of salt, or maybe a big pinch: "I find in the order-taking model, what you think you want to know is actually not what you need to know. Sometimes the conversation starts, 'I want to do a product test; or I need a CLT; I need a triangle test.' And my inner voice goes, 'Do you?'"

She often must play detective to get to the underlying problem. "So, two of my favorite sleuths are Columbo and Poirot. Columbo's like, 'Another thing . . . I'm sorry . . . I know I'm bugging you, but one more thing.' He's intentionally annoying. He plays like he doesn't know he's annoying, but he's intentionally being annoying. And so, therefore, that will get people to respond to you in a certain way, so you need some thick skin."

"On the other hand, I love the Belgian sleuth, Poirot. He uses his little grey cells. Sometimes, I've got to sit back and be quiet and just observe, and watch and listen, because maybe we don't even need to make a request. Maybe we don't even need to do the research. Or maybe the request for the research has nothing to do with the problem. And that's why, if somebody comes to me and says, 'Hey, I want to do some focus groups,' I'll just go: 'Do you?'"

This probing and questioning takes some boldness. Sauriol says, "I think it is our job to push and probe and ask the difficult questions. And force people to demonstrate why this request is something we should do." He finds it's necessary to push back because stakeholders are often seeing their problem from the perspective of "their very narrow slice of the business, and the world that they live in. They are trying to solve for X when, in reality, it's a lot bigger than that."

This need to push back is not without costs. Jila Bick, of the pharmaceutical company Sunovion, inherited a culture of order taking when she joined as Executive Director, Commercial Analytics. She turned that around, as we'll see later in this chapter. Some of her stakeholders found the change difficult to take.

I used to work with Jila. She is not one to back down. And neither is she out to win popularity contests, if she thinks it is at the expense of doing the right thing. Her perspective is "at the end of the day we are not doing the business a favor by capitulating on areas that are fundamental to the business or the brand," even though stakeholders, she says, "may not want to have lunch with you."

Anamaria Gotelli, former Consumer & Market Knowledge at P&G and Estée Lauder Companies and currently Marketing Director of Estée Lauder in Paris takes a similar stance. "I was not there to listen to what they wanted to do in terms of research," she declares. "I was telling them what is needed, and I was defining the agenda because it was my responsibility."

That's the future of insights.

Education is a responsibility

"I think the insights function needs to take a role in terms of educating folks, and senior folks, on what to do, and get them forward-looking," proposes Michael Haynes, author and principal of Australia's 2Excell Consulting. But there is, he suggests, often a lack of understanding at the top. Its effects are then exacerbated by a power imbalance. That makes it difficult for the insights team.

"In many big organizations," he says, "their true value and potential is not leveraged well. It's misunderstood. I find senior execs seem to find the latest buzzword, and then they jump onto it. Net promoter score—now it's all about CX. They'll jump onto whatever they hear, and then they jump onto that metric because everyone wants 'the data,' 'the number.'"

He has seen a lot of direction from the top being, "'This is what we need; make it happen.' So, even when the insights team is trying to say, 'Well, the business should have . . .' they're not really given that opportunity. They're just told, 'This is how it is in our world. Go forth. Make it happen. Want it yesterday. And no, you can't have any more people.'"

Even in those kinds of difficult circumstances, the insights leaders of tomorrow have an obligation to lead the way by educating their stakeholders. U.S. Bank's Vidya Subramani says, "I feel a lot of our problems come because we have not educated corporate leadership in truly understanding the process, the initial investigatory process before we start saying, 'Oh, let's just ask this question and get an answer.'"

Twitter's Kishibe says, "It's our role to educate the marketing team, to say, 'Actually we can do a lot more than that' . . . We always strip it right back. 'What are you trying to do?' 'Give us that context.' Because usually those types of people don't come to us with context. It's like, 'Hey, Maggie, I'm wondering if you have any stats that say that Twitter users think we're fun?' And I'm not going to answer that question. We flat out won't answer. And so, we'll step back, and we'll say, 'Okay, I need a little bit more context. Let's meet. Tell me where this request is coming from.'"

"I think that Twitter is starting to change for the better," she says, "in that the more we have these conversations with the marketers, the more they start to see: 'Okay, I don't have to actually tell you what question to ask. But I can tell you the objective, and you will give me the best recommendation.' That's a shift in the organization."

Elizabeth Moore, Director of Research, Insights and Analytics at Telstra in Australia, has made getting to the root of the business question a crucial part of what the team does. "We've had the team put through some training on 'asking excellent questions' just this week," she explains. This is particularly crucial given the nature of her organization. "We're a large, complex matrix organization, and a project very rarely has just one stakeholder, one business person that we're doing it for. It's usually a consortium across the business. You need to be able to get clarity on what is the real business problem that you're trying to solve, rather than 'go and get me this data.'"

When you can break through to the root problem, the discussion becomes more interactive and more fruitful. Sauriol describes it this way: "You're talking about the issue. You're all on the same page. You're thinking about it from a business impact standpoint. You've got different points of view represented at the table and you've got a whole roundtable, if you will, of people who are primarily focused on addressing this issue, or solving this question."

That is far more productive, and more fun, than just taking an order, or wasting time playing detective.

Start taking action

The insights professionals of the future will not just do interesting studies. They will be finding business solutions. They will be taking actions that generate revenue, not thinking of ideas to be explored. That's not always the case right now.

If you are focused on making a difference in the business, and not just doing a "cool study," putting methodology first is unhelpful. Gotelli says she is not interested in hearing about data because "the business doesn't sell data." She is interested in hearing about solutions to business problems, not what a study found.

Researchers are often intoxicated by the methodology of their studies and are not as focused on what they mean to the business. Gotelli says, "there are a lot of researchers who are passionate about analysis, passionate about data, without necessarily looking for what's going to be the impact in the business." That doesn't cut it anymore. "Researchers now have to be better about driving executions, beyond just collecting the data," says Howard Shimmel, former CRO of Time Warner's Turner unit.

"Tell me what is important, not what you found," U.S. Bank's Vidya Subramani says. It is not just in-house researchers she pushes to change: "I still struggle with that with many of my vendor partners. For them, it's moving beyond, 'Oh, this is what the customers told us.' But what does it mean? We need much more of a focus on 'What does it mean?'" Similarly, Telstra's Moore says that for her, the bottom line for all research is "What are you going to do differently as a result of knowing this?"

The insights professionals of the future need to be more about business than about research. They cannot be the "little grey mice" taking orders. They need to understand the business, be embedded in it, and make sure their voice is heard, loud and clear. Peter Harris, EVP & Managing Director of Asia Pacific at Vision Critical, says, "I think it's about being familiar with what we're trying to achieve as a business, and then, 'How can I use the data that I have access to to be able to prove a point or make better decisions?'"

Howard Shimmel is a research veteran, so I asked him what he would say to young people just starting out. "I would say try to learn the business: to be 80 percent as fluent as your internal clients are," he suggested. "Because you can't be a researcher in a vacuum anymore—we need to be more embedded in the business." We'll see examples of how that can work later in this chapter when we look at the stories of companies like Sunovion Pharmaceuticals, World Vision Canada, Virgin Australia and TD.

Without an in-depth appreciation of the business on the part of insights professionals, research can not only be unhelpful, its credibility can be undermined. Greco finds it exceptionally frustrating "when research, even trying to deliver insights, will misunderstand the context of the business. The researcher says, for example, 'You know, this show is great, but viewers don't like the main character. The main character needs to be re-cast.' And you are like, 'Yeah, but we shot the whole show, and we are sitting in post-production. That's not possible.' You are dead on arrival. The reaction to anything else you say after that is going to be 'this guy doesn't understand the business.'"

That kind of misstep gives insights a bad name, even if the research was brilliant.

Delivering commercial outcomes

The voice of insights is more likely to be heard and understood if we stop using the language of research. Insights must stop being perceived as a cost center, and start being understood as delivering clear commercial value.

Peter Harris draws a direct line between our ability to demonstrate financial benefit and having a voice at the table: "We haven't been relevant enough, or good enough about articulating the impact of investment in insights. We haven't been able to link that to hard sales performance within organizations. I think that once we can link it to sales databases, once you can really become more accountable—for something across more than one data set within the business—then you've actually got power." Stevens agrees: "What they really need to see is how the research translates to commercial value. This focus on value is a very different proposition to project managing, tracking programs, or that kind of role."

ESOMAR's Raben suggests, "One of the themes that tends to be front of mind for many global insights leaders is return on investment. I think that insights departments, within brand owners or end clients, are going to either succeed or fail depending on how they can articulate that return on investment."

Return on investment is what interests the senior leadership team. "Companies that have an insights champion at the board level appear to thrive," Raben says. He referenced i2020, a study whose results were published in the *Harvard Business Review*, September 2016: "The i2020 research shows that insights leaders in overperforming organizations report to these [C-level] senior executives more than twice as often as their counterparts in underperforming organizations do (29% versus 12%)."

Stop being a researcher, and start being a fully informed decision maker

"The demands of the insights profession, moving forward, are very different from what was needed when we all came into the industry," Raben notes. "That does have implications for the skill sets that we require."

The skill set for the insights professional of the future will be radically expanded. A solid grasp of methodology, statistics, sociology and psychology will not be enough. The ability to comprehend cultural context, digital marketing, history, and predictive analytics will also be essential—as will the skill to synthesize these inputs into a simple message of what Haynes calls: "So what? What's next?"

Telstra's Moore says that, for her team, the skills needed have already changed. "It is quite a different skill set. It's not just 'pull somebody out of a research house and plug them into the team.'" She needs people who can extract insights from, and know when to use, multiple types of information.

"You need to be able to tell a story. You need to be able to string information together. You need to be able to look at the data lake, understand it, and understand what qual you need to wrap around that. You need an understanding of social media sentiment tracking, and when to use it, and when to commission traditional qual. You need to understand the business too. I think that we will see more people in insights roles coming from strategy companies, people who understand the way businesses work, and understand how to read a balance sheet, and what free cash flow is, and why EBITDA is important."

"You must have this mindset of being a consultant while aiming to be fully integrated to the business," says Gotelli, "and look for solutions in a way that is easy to understand, like The Boston Consulting Group and McKinsey." Shimmel agrees with that, but also thinks the consultant qualities need to be coupled with other hard skills. "If I could ever build the ideal researcher, I would clone someone who's a third McKinsey consultant, a third data scientist, and a third someone who's got the current research skills and instincts, who is concerned about the quality of data, and who knows how to do surveys, to explore complex issues that you can't address through big data."

This requires a stretch from where we are at today, but it's not exactly a foreign endeavor. Stevens points out, "There's a bigger range of data sources but, effectively, we're talking about the scientific method. We're developing a hypothesis, and we're going to try and find the data points to prove or disprove it. I think the range of different data sources is independent from the sort of skills needed to go and make decisions and influence things."

A need for ongoing education

Researchers must pick up new skills and become familiar with other methods. "The insights people that I see who are future-proofing themselves are getting their heads around digital marketing skills, analytics, data science and technology," says Stevens. "They have an understanding, even if it's not highly detailed, that enables them to talk the talk effectively. And they see how those methods get used alongside traditional research approaches in a source-agnostic way."

Picking up these new skills requires a significant investment in continuing education, which shockingly few insights professionals are currently making. According to Ray Poynter and Sue York's #NewMR *Market Research Knowledge Benchmarking Study 2018,* 38% of market researchers had 5 hours or less of training in the past 12 months. Poynter and York conclude, ". . . too many market researchers are not receiving enough training, something which we believe is endangering the future of market research as a knowledge-based, value-adding industry and profession."

Shimmel encouraged ongoing learning at Turner by arranging for people in the insights department to get some exposure to other techniques. "Turner's campus in Atlanta is right next to Georgia State," he explained. "I connected with someone in their data science group, who ran a training program for us. We put 50 people through advanced data management skills. We were starting to train people on how to use SAS and SPSS—how to tap into data lakes and things like that." He recognizes that that is not enough. "We need to train them on skills like that," he says, "but we also need to train them on how to walk the walk, and talk the talk, like someone from McKinsey."

ESOMAR's Raben doesn't see higher education as being responsive to this need for more well-rounded training—yet. "When you look around different universities—and I'm fortunate enough to be involved with a number of them across different regions—they're still quite traditional in their approach." He thinks there is a need to offer a broader education that looks beyond traditional quantitative and qualitative research because areas like anthropology, digital marketing, history, and predictive analytics are "the skill sets that we need developed."

Raben believes market researchers are well positioned to make this leap: "I think we are still the best data manipulators and managers around, because it's in our blood." But he recognizes that we must act quickly and decisively. "If we don't adapt some of our teaching and training going forward, we may well be left behind."

The #NewMR numbers probably overestimate the percentage of researchers who do continuing education—because those who are fully detached from learning are probably not tapped into education centers like #NewMR. That's disheartening because it suggests this lack of change will lead to a significant culling of the herd. But maybe that's a good thing for the evolution of the insights function.

We've seen that the insights function started out as a handmaiden to marketing and advertising and is shifting from order taker to agenda setter. That requires educating people about how research can be planned and what it can deliver. It also involves a relentless focus on taking action to deliver tangible commercial benefits, not just having interesting findings. Doing this effectively means adopting a more business-centered, consultative mindset. It also requires more learning, both in getting deeper into the business and in picking up new skills to be able to deal with a wider array of information sources.

In the last part of this chapter, we'll look at the stories of four different insights groups and how they have been transforming their functions. Each has undergone unique revolutions, but they all illustrate aspects of the changes and challenges we have seen thus far.

Sunovion Pharmaceuticals: from data processors to agenda setters

Sunovion is a pharmaceutical company that makes medications like Lunesta, Omnaris and Alvesco. Jila Bick is Executive Director, Commercial Analytics. After many years on the supplier side, specializing in healthcare, she joined Boehringer Ingelheim's analytics team and moved through the ranks to the role of Executive Director, reshaping the research department along the way. When she moved over to Sunovion, she says, she "inherited a team that was perceived to be a data dump organization. It was all about just sending Excel files, and sending tables with a bunch of numbers. And the team didn't provide a lot of insight around the numbers, and didn't implement what it meant for the business."

Prior to her joining, the company had done benchmarking for the whole of commercial operations, including Commercial Analytics. "When I came in, they gave me the results of the benchmarking, and the report card was awful for Commercial Analytics. We didn't do much competitive insight; our reports didn't have any management summary or key takeaways; 20 percent of the work we did was primary market research and there was a high, high level of reliance on just pure number crunching."

The unit was a team in name only. They were embedded within marketing teams, with people sitting with specific products or categories. "There was no sense of team cohesiveness, team synergy, or sharing best practices. The people who were doing secondary analysis didn't talk to the people who were doing primary market research on behalf of the brand. And even within a brand, one person was in charge of patient insights, and one person was in charge of physician research. They didn't talk to each other. They didn't participate in each other's research. They didn't share information. It was very fragmented in terms of analytics—bits and pieces—mostly pieces."

They were order takers. "When I took over," Bick explains, "it was 90 percent ad hoc, 10 percent planned." The ad hoc work was responding to marketers' requests. And there was no plan—just a budget per brand. But senior management had an appetite for change.

The leadership wanted "people who think strategically, think out of the box, focusing not just on delivering numbers but on what these numbers mean to the business—people who are proactive and bring ideas to the table. There was a list of things they wanted to do, and they were all good. So, we said 'all right.'" And thus, the transformation began.

"The first thing we decided to do was to reverse the order, to come up with many more preplanned activities, rather than just try to manage the ad hoc requests over time." While this sounds straightforward, it led to some headbutting with marketers who were used to getting what they wanted, when they wanted. Bick found that marketers—especially those with just enough research knowledge to be dangerous—needed to be educated on how to use research proactively rather than reactively. They also needed to learn that there was a sequence to learning about a market and a product, and that you could not skip foundational steps.

"I think it's hard," Bick says, "especially if you have an uneducated, or not fully educated, marketing customer who tends to prefer the sexy part of the analytics. They want to take shortcuts on the things that are fundamental to develop their communication platform." She found that when they did not do the foundational work first, "they created all these creative concepts that they put in front of the physicians, and the physicians laughed their heads off. I'm wasting money, because you really need to wait to find out what the physicians really want out of this treatment area, what they are lacking, and what is important. We reinforced the fact that in order to do positioning or messaging—all the sexy stuff that marketers like to do—you need to do strategic work up front: identifying your targets customers, your market size. You profile your segments and come up with the drivers and barriers."

"This is a very delicate balance between trying to educate the marketing customer, making sure they understand, and prioritizing the work," she explains. "You need to do a lot of negotiation, and make sure that they understand the importance of investing money in different areas."

The insights staff also needed education on putting a focus on storytelling, providing recommendations, and using multiple data sources—not relying on the results of one study. The change was hard for some. She told the team, "If you want to be number crunchers, there is no future for us. We have to change. Otherwise, they will get rid of our jobs." "Some people didn't want to," she says, "or they didn't have the capabilities, or they felt that that was not what they signed up for, so eventually they moved on."

She also pushed the team to focus on making a commercial difference: "No matter what we do or how we do it, we have to showcase our value. We have to show that we have an impact on the business."

The transformation has been considerable, but obviously not without hard work and challenges. I asked Jila if she had any advice for other people who are facing change. She said, "Stay focused. Don't give up. It's hard." But change through education, co-operation and learning new skills has its rewards too. She said, "when I look at this team, and how the members tackle different areas, it has come a long way. It has a ways to go. But it has come a long way."

World Vision: insights driving a holistic view of the customer, and a change in structure

Elias Hadaya joined World Vision Canada as Director, Insight and Research in 2011, after spending time in the worlds of telecommunications and financial services. He was attracted by the charity's purpose and cause. When he joined, Hadaya started a review and transformation of the insights department. Now he has the role of Vice President Customer Experience, and the organization views, and acts on, donors holistically. This is a story of an organizational transformation, driven by insights.

When he joined World Vision, Hadaya "booked meetings with every colleague, every tier—and also with the senior leadership team. I did the same with every member of the research team, not only the managers. And I asked two questions, the same questions for the two audiences. My first question was: 'Do you believe that we need, at World Vision Canada, to have an insights and research team?' The second one was: 'Can you tell me what is the unique value that this team is bringing to the work that we do at World Vision Canada?'"

"So, the first question was asking if I needed to do this job; do we need to invest in an insight and research team? Everyone from the two audiences said, 'Of course, Elias. We need the numbers. We need the team. It's a competitive advantage.' It was very good to hear agreement around such an important role and team. The answer to the second question was fuzzier. People couldn't pinpoint the unique value of the team. They knew that the team had value, but they didn't know what that value was."

"I received several anecdotes around 'Oh yes, I ask for a report, I get the report.' 'Oh yes, they did the campaigns lists—they do that well actually.' 'And the quality is good, and they are very responsive.' But nobody could pinpoint the unique value. And when I asked the same question of my team members, they said, 'Well, we can actually do far more, but nobody is asking.' So, from that point, I knew what I needed to do. We needed to shift the department from a request-driven department, to a full domain of expertise."

Hadaya saw four things the team needed to start doing. The first was "becoming a true business partner." That meant "engage the organization, to challenge the business partners to work hand-in-hand with the rest of the business." The second was "producing insights rather than data." He told the team, "It's not good enough to say: 'This is the report'…or even to say, 'I looked at the data and this is what the data is telling me.'" He was looking to the team to provide "prescriptive recommendations. And I'm not talking about the last slide in a PowerPoint," he laughed. His vision was to "start with what your understanding is and then go to the data. Start with the end."

The third step was to develop a deep understanding of the business, so the team could make informed recommendations. Earlier, we heard Michael Greco point out how ill-informed recommendations undermine the credibility of research. Hadaya echoed this point when he told the team, "If you are doing a direct mail analysis, and you don't know direct mail, then please don't do a direct mail analysis." He challenged the team: "Don't just be a provider, a broker of data."

The fourth new requirement turned out to be the most impactful: to have a "holistic view of the market and the consumer." In his review, Hadaya said, the insights staff told him: "'Well, the business is very 'siloed.' Everyone comes to us with one piece, and then we have another team that asks a similar question, but through another lens. And we end up doing multiple things . . . with the same target audience, but nobody sees the big picture." "For instance," he explained, "the channel team is interested in direct mail analysis, and then you have the revenue folks, the folks who are looking at how much we missed the revenue, and they are interested in the revenue analysis piece."

Faced with this truth, Hadaya took the perspective that the insights function should see itself as having "carte blanche." "I know my job description, I know my performance appraisal targets, and all that. In my 20 years of experience, I have observed that nobody tells you how you're going to do it. I'm the captain of my ship, and every analyst is the captain of their own analysis. They have way more freedom than they believe they have."

With this philosophy in mind, Hadaya said to his team, "There is no one else that has a position to see this holistic view. Our team is empowered to see the bigger picture."

He said, "We responded to the challenge by transforming the function." As a result, the organization "recognized that we cannot be organized around products and channels. Our new structure is organized around customers and integration."

Now, as Vice President of Customer Experience, Hadaya ensures donors and prospects are viewed and acted on holistically: "These are the three pillars of our marketing strategy: to diversify audience, to build the brand, and to diversify revenue." "Inside that," he says, "the Customer Experience division is really the enabler of that transformation, in collaboration with our internal stakeholders."

"Another title that can explain better what my team and I are doing is 'Business Transformation.' We are looking at how we are connecting the donors from a front-page perspective: what the consumer is feeling; what are the emotions; how they are perceiving our brand; what is the brand promise, are we delivering on that? When they go on the website, what kind of experience do they have?

This is a great example of how stopping taking orders, and starting to take action, can transform the organization itself.

Virgin Australia: an agenda focused on driving business

Steven Cierpicki was a supplier-side researcher in Australia for many years before joining Virgin Australia, an airline, as Manager, Research and Customer Insights. He recently spearheaded a reformation of the insights function. His team has moved from being an order taker to becoming an agenda setter with a very singular focus: generating growth in the business. This change has revolutionized the type of work they do, the tools they use, and the suppliers they work with.

When Cierpicki first joined, he says, "Our modus operandi was like a little research agency within a business. We would take orders. We'd ask: 'Right, what do you want to do?' And we were really good at that. We built up a huge reputation across the business, and everyone liked giving us briefs."

But he could see that each group that was commissioning them was quite siloed, and only looked at things from their own perspective. "Our business is probably similar to others," he says, "in that if you work in the food space, then your belief is that food is most important, and if you work in cabin crew, then you think cabin crew service is the most important thing. If you work in the lounges, you think lounges are really important, and if you work in technology, you think that the e-commerce side is most important. And then, on top of that, there's just the operational side, which is: 'I need more people to work for the baggage handling area,' or 'I need more people to work at check-in desks,' or 'I need more whatever it is.'"

The problem with that model, he says, was that "no one really knows what is actually delivering customer outcomes. What is it that ultimately a business is trying to do around the customer? We decided that our insights team in Virgin Australia wasn't just going to be a really awesome service provider. We took a really strong perspective that we wanted to be directive of the agenda."

They believed that the insights team should lead the way by being "really focused on what things will attract people to fly with us, or

keep people flying with us, and then increasing their share of wallet."
Ultimately, the specific agenda was "How do we become a more
successful business commercially through delivering better customer-
centric outcomes?"

To do this, they needed to set the agenda. Cierpicki says, "I pitched it
to my new executive, Tash. I said to her, 'Look. I want to start our
team stepping up and being directive. When someone comes and
offers us a brief and says, "Can we do research?" we might push
back, or say, "No, that's not important." What we need to do is have a
knowledge agenda.' Fortunately, Tash agreed with that, and we've
now got a program of strategic research that's forming knowledge."

That's a revolutionary stance that required backing from the CEO on
down. And it involved a change in structure, with insights quite
literally getting a seat at the table. He explains that his boss "reports
to the Chief Executive Officer of the Virgin Australia business. And
she's not an insights person. She's an operational manager, but has
always had a customer focus. And before airlines, she was in hotels.
She really knows the importance of, and really believes in, that
customer-centric way of operating. She was prepped to speak to the
CEO. And through those discussions, the CEO started what's called a
Customer Board."

On this Board, "There's the CEO. And there's my manager—who's
head of customer experience and product development. And then
there's me. And then there's a head ground operation person, and the
head of technology. So, through that Customer Board, I've got
influence across the business."

With that kind of backing, Cierpicki says, "our team just sat down
and said, 'These are the most important questions the business needs
to answer.' And that's the directive approach. Once you figure out
'What does the business need to answer?' you can start to push down
that path, rather than waiting for a brief to come in."

The team's singular focus on the financial outcome of decisions
makes the agenda very clear. "We started a knowledge agenda, in
which the fundamental question is: 'What drives customers to choose
Virgin Australia?' We're framing it from a financial perspective. We

put a value on what is the share of wallet of the existing fly base. The same from an acquisition point of view: we looked at the entire market and the value of a group of people that have not flown with us, and how many there are, and what the value of that is. I think framing it as a financial opportunity is really critical."

This focus on growth caused the Virgin Australia insights team to rethink who their primary research supplier should be. "We found a supplier who is like-minded," Cierpicki says. This company has "taken the path of becoming strategic growth consultants." They are "aligned to that agenda of everything you report back on is about: 'Is this success?' as opposed to just interesting facts and figures."

The result of the insights team setting the agenda has been positive. "We've gotten more kudos and more respect," he explains, "because we are actually helping."

TD: from siloed suggestions to integrated action

When I spoke to Meghan Nameth, she had left her post as TD's head of North American Marketing Analytics and Insights the week before. She had left to become Co-Founder and Co-CEO of iVirtual Technologies. Prior to that she was VP of Personal Banking at TD and had worked as a marketer in various consumer goods manufacturers, including P&G and Mars. The analytics role at TD was her first foray into the world of insights—and she brought to it a restlessness for action.

"When I took on the research and insights function," she recounts, "they were set up in functional silos. We had an advanced analytics team, a research insights team, campaign analytics, and a list team. Everyone had this very deep functional expertise. Which sounds great because you can build out great technical capability. But what you tradeoff is the business partnership." In this siloed environment, she says, "The business doesn't know who in the insights function they go to with their biggest problem, which is typically: 'How do I generate more revenue?' or: 'How do I make more money? Or drive out cost?'"

At the same time, the analytics people were frustrated. "They would do these great reports, or create these great analytics or insights, and then the business wouldn't take them seriously or wouldn't change what they were doing." The insights team felt they were "disconnected from the business problems. And the business didn't know where they could get the most help." The marketers didn't know "who could look at the business problem and give them a unique solution." Nameth could see change was needed.

She saw the solution in creating a new type of role, an evolution of the insights function. This new role was one of identifying business problems, and then matching the problem to the skill set available within analytics. "What I really started doing," she says, "was looking at more of a horizontal/vertical structure where you could say: 'We're going to have insights and analytics leaders that are more generalists in their skill set, and able to really participate at the leadership level. But we're also going to assemble cross-functional teams that would deliver innovative solutions." These people become a horizontal layer, connecting the vertical specializations. She made the necessary changes—which were significant.

"I was able to go to each of the business leaders and say, 'You're going to have a dedicated person on your team that's going to bring you all of the expertise of the analytics and research department to help you with your business. Your goals are going to be their goals.'"

This job was: "If the problem we're experiencing is, for example, we do not consolidate enough of our customers' wealth, and we lose share of wallet to other competitors, then what team would I draw on? Do we not understand the consumer barrier? Could we create a predictive analytics model to solve this? Or could we present information to the customer in a different way? Do we need to generate a leads program for our advisors?'"

Finding the people who could fill this role was challenging because it required a broad understanding of what analytics could deliver, coupled with a deep knowledge of the business. "It's a different skill set for sure," she says. "We had some in our department already that were able to tell a story, understand the problem, influence at the leadership level, and really understand enough of the analytics that they knew the right questions to ask the deep functional experts."

She says the business was pleased with the change: her stakeholders were "absolutely thrilled because they finally had one person to go to, rather than five different people and having to decide. They always wanted much more holistic support, and they were yearning for the partnership and the connection. It was very well received."

Not everyone is suited for this consultant role, she suggests. "I think there are analytics people who are dying to get closer to the business, and there are analytics people who are dying to stay purely in the math." The challenge is finding those "people who say, 'Yeah, I love the analytics, but I really like it when my analytics is connected, and I can be in the business conversations.'" "And those people are absolutely there. You just have to find them," she says. "I think we need to be more open to people who don't have a pure functional background. I don't have a math degree, but I'm able to follow along with the thinking. I can't build the model, but I can certainly follow along with the logic and ask the right questions."

Critical to the success of this function, she said, is to be able to translate the insights into action. "Once you get the output, you need to translate it back to the business to say: 'Okay, here's what we created, and here's why it solves your problem; here's what it will do differently for you.' It's the 'so what' and then 'now what you should go do about it.'" She says, "We really need to take it to: 'This is what it means, and this is what it will do for you.'"

The logical extension of that, she believes, is not to recommend changes, but to create change. The idea is not to be a research department and test ideas, but instead to become a research and development group. "The shift that we were making was to set up an experimentation lab where we run new marketing programs, do A/B tests in a controlled environment. Then we can prove out new results, and start to put new programs on the shelf, so that when we have an opening, we can run them at scale."

This shift from just research to research and development required the addition of new skills to the team. "In order to run an experiment,"

Nameth explains, "you have to create new marketing materials, you have to actually put them in market, then measure the results." She wanted to know, "'What would be true if we ran it at scale?' Typically, an insights or research team has not gone that deep. We've had to add new capability to the experiment team. Basically, bringing in marketing communications experts, strategy and business experts, to help round out the skill set. That's where I think research needs to go; it needs to be much more executional and run more like an experiment lab."

She believes "An R&D unit is what the insights function needs to evolve to. It's less about being research as a paperwork exercise, and much more about being hands-on, and able to understand, 'How do I get to a prototype? And then what is the response? And then how would I refine it?'"

This approach is but one excellent example of how insights can move beyond taking orders, and start taking action.

Chapter 3 - Stop Analyzing in Isolation and Start Thinking Outside the Survey

"He blew it." Did he make a mistake that led to failure? Or are we learning how he created a beautiful glass vase?

Context is everything.

Consider, for example, the black dot below. What is it?

•

Is it the moon in eclipse? Or is it a tiny black hole—a gravitational field so intense that nothing can escape its pull? Or is it the black dot from *Treasure Island* that so terrified the pirate Billy Bones he had a stroke and died? Or is it simply the dot at the bottom of a question mark, found at the end of this sentence?

A wonderful example of the importance of contextualization comes from British philosopher Gilbert Ryle. In a 1968 lecture, Ryle stated, "Two boys fairly swiftly contract the eyelids of their right eyes. In the first boy this is only an involuntary twitch; but the other is winking conspiratorially to an accomplice. At the lowest or the thinnest level of description the two contractions of the eyelids may be exactly alike. From a cinematograph-film of the two faces there might be no telling which contraction, if either, was a wink, or which, if either, was a mere twitch. Yet there remains the immense but unphotographable difference between a twitch and a wink." Ryle called this a "thick" description, one that has multiple layers of information.

A true insight cannot be born in isolation. A single result can give you an answer to a question. "The ad passed our benchmark" is an answer, but it is not an insight. The Cambridge Dictionary has a useful definition of insight: "a clear, deep, and sometimes sudden understanding of a complicated problem or situation."

A depth of understanding comes from having multiple pieces of information. The insight comes from how you connect those pieces. Ada Lovelace wrote the first computer science paper in 1843, and collaborated with Charles Babbage to invent the first computer. She believed insights came from the power of making connections. She wrote that imagination "brings together things, facts, ideas, conceptions, in new, original, endless, ever varying, combinations. It seizes points in common, between subjects having no very apparent connexion, & hence seldom or never brought into juxtaposition."

Steve Jobs made a similar point about the power of connections. "Creativity is just connecting things. When you ask creative people how they did something, they feel a little guilty because they didn't really do it, they just saw something. It seemed obvious to them after a while. That's because they were able to connect experiences they've had and synthesize new things."

If context is so obviously important, why are so many studies commissioned and executed in complete isolation? Most research reports include no information other than what comes out of the survey. And most requests for research come with only the scantest of background information and almost no sense of how the research problem fits into a brand's or organization's bigger picture. By doing this, we handicap ourselves. We risk misunderstanding what we think is the answer, and fail to deliver the best insights possible.

"One of the weirdest things that market researchers do is present a report or debrief that is based solely on the piece of research they have just conducted," says Ray Poynter, Founder and Chair of the #NewMR. "What amazing hubris to assume that your research project on its own is going to answer any meaningful question." Hubris is an exceptionally apt word for Poynter to use because it highlights the danger of lacking context.

Hubris is a word that comes to English from Ancient Greece. It describes how overweening pride or self-confidence leads to downfall and death. Think Achilles, Oedipus, and Icarus flying too close to the sun. Hubris is a toxic combination of ignorance and overestimation.

When we focus on the results of a single study, without context, we are, at best, missing an opportunity for greater insights. At worst, we can ignorantly provide "insights" that are misleading. It happens all the time.

The study is the solution

The tendency to treat the results of a single study as a satisfactory answer to a research problem has multiple roots. They include a history where primary research was often the only data source, a need for speed, silos within organizations, and a heritage of having worked on the supplier side—where money is made by doing one-off surveys or focus groups.

In the past, if you wanted to know what people watched or listened to, you had to ask them. If you wanted to discover what groceries they bought, you had to ask them. And if you wanted to identify where people shopped, you had to ask them. But now, we are inundated with behavioral data. There are many sources that are quite accurate at measuring what people do, buy and consume. Yes, they have their limitations and their blind spots, but so do people who answer surveys. Still, old habits die hard.

People raised in the world of market research tend to default to doing surveys—because it's relatively fast and easy. Eleonora Jonusiene, Director of International Consumer Insights & Research at Warner

Bros Home Entertainment, says she has often seen researchers "rush to the field with a new study, instead of analyzing what we already know based on the previous primary research or syndicated research, because we do not have time to go through the historical information."

Ihno Froehling, who currently handles Global Respiratory Marketing Insights & Strategy at GSK in Switzerland, agrees. "We have a lot of data in different places," he says. "It's not yet a reality that you can bring the information together easily. It's typically very time-consuming for us to do that. It's often easier and faster to call up the supplier and start a new research study than to try to make sense of the myriad of existing data and insights that you have. It's a sad fact." This need for speed often goes hand in hand with the reactive order-giving mentality that we looked at in the previous chapter.

The order-giving approach to insights sees research as a means to an end. It answers the question "Did you test this ad?": "Yes, and it passed the benchmark." It does not embody a more holistic approach where you first comprehend what drives purchasing, then craft a message that resonates, and then convert that understanding into a campaign that drives those messages home. It is a reductionist tactic that encourages thinking about research as a one-off exercise, rather than a cumulative journey of understanding.

This short-sighted approach is endemic to the traditional buyer-supplier relationship. If studies are commissioned on a one-off basis, the contextual information suppliers have is very limited. They might get a brief that has a high-level description of the market, but it is very rare to be given a meaningful understanding of the offer, or the marketplace. That only occurs when there are deep, ongoing relationships: where the supplier becomes part of the team. A procurement-driven, project-by-project approach results in suppliers being forced to act in relative isolation. Unfortunately, that is not uncommon.

Jonusiene points out that the "majority of marketing researchers have joined business organizations from the research agencies," where they were order takers—who typically work on a study-by-study basis. This single study orientation biases them to "continue to behave as agents or order takers"—people who default to seeing a single study as the solution. Thus, the problem perpetuates itself.

"You know the saying: 'If all you have is a hammer, everything looks like a nail?'" says Lucid's Patrick Comer. "Researchers are like that. They answer everything with a survey. The reality is there may be simple social data, or you can just log onto Google analytics and glean information that is free and already there. You can then start driving the next level of insights out of that."

But this isn't just a problem with surveys. It is the same with any single dataset—including big data. "I think we've all gotten a little bit mesmerized," says Howard Shimmel. "Big data and first-party data is great, but it does provide a limited view of the world. I think we've got to do a better job of integrating survey data, panel data, first-party data, and being clear about how it all comes together to provide a solution."

U.S. Bank's Vidya Subramani told me a story about a behavioral analysis that underscores this point: "The company did some data analysis to understand why a certain group of customers were not using their credit card. They said, 'Okay, let's do some behavioral analysis.' And they looked at the data and found that those who were not using their credit cards had lower credit limits than those who were using their credit cards. So, 'Aha! The problem is credit limits. Let's increase the credit limits, and then they'll start using the card.'"

She suggested that the marketers talk to customers and figure out what kind of credit limit they needed. "When we spoke to those customers, the majority said, 'I didn't even know I had this credit card. I didn't sign up for this credit card.'" It turned out these customers had automatically been given the card when they signed up for a checking account. "They hadn't asked for the product. There wasn't a need for the product. Giving them a greater credit line would not make them start using the card."

It was, she recounts, "one of those 'Aha' moments when they realized that they do need market research. The two approaches go hand in hand."

Lack of context can be a zombie nightmare

A good friend of mine is a researcher and strategist who works in a B2B environment where there are relatively few customers. Each customer is quite valuable—if they use your product. She was asked to track the change in a small and complex market. Having never worked in this space before, she reluctantly inherited someone else's study—and didn't like the way some of the questions were worded. So, she improved them.

The request for proposal had some boilerplate background on the product, but nothing about the market dynamics, the history of the product, or the target customers. The commissioning researcher was minimally forthcoming when asked questions and was "too busy" to provide a proper briefing. With no choice but to move forward to meet a tight deadline, my friend launched the study, with a sample of 30 current and potential customers. It was a tiny sample, but it was the maximum number of people who could be surveyed.

The results came back, and they were radically unlike the prior wave. Perceptions of the brand were completely different, and some of the key indicators had changed as much as 30%. She checked and rechecked the data, scouring it for outliers. Had she surveyed an unrepresentative sample? Was a sample of 30 just too small to track anything? Had a couple of wording changes made a difference? With uncertainty playing on her subconscious, she had a nightmare about bad data—the morning before she was to review the findings with her client.

As she nervously went over some of the key findings and queried her client about what they thought about this radical change in the market, she was met with a shrug and "yeah, that's exactly what we expected." Asked why she had not shared that before, the client said, "Oh, we didn't want to bias you."

Besides being insulted by the lack of trust, my friend was angry at the lost potential. How much better could the study have been if that had been known? How might that knowledge have led to a refocusing of the investigation? Or a different angle on the analysis? Or even just a decent night's sleep? The tiniest sliver of context could have cast a whole new light on the problem.

Sadly, I have heard that story, or variations of it, too many times. It was a case of, "Oh, we should track that," tragically paired with a distracted commissioning researcher who could not be bothered to be a strategic partner.

Studies like that are like zombies. They are half dead and half alive, stumbling forward blindly. Oh yes, the tracking was done, and the box ticked. But at what cost? What do studies like that do to the reputation of the insights function?

No doubt the product manager duly noted that tracking confirmed what they already knew—the market had changed. It was an opportunity squandered, all for lack of context.

What does the . mean?

There is danger in having a blinkered approach, and great value in thinking about a business problem contextually. "I can see a data point, and we can have 1,000,001 different perspectives on what that means to the business, but ultimately it means nothing," according to Visa's Kristopher Sauriol. "It's just pure speculation unless we have additional data or knowledge."

He believes "You need to layer on other information to get a firm understanding of what's happening. To me, that means there is a qualitative component, syndicated data we have available to us, and in-market observations. All these are critical for us to be able to decide what a data point means."

Using multiple information sources also encourages people to look at the big picture, and not be intoxicated by numbers and charts. When you synthesize multiple sources of information, it enforces a focus on summarizing the results as a story. It does not lend itself to producing a 100-page deck of charts. It encourages a 4-page summary of what to do next.

Who saw the gorilla in the room?

One of the challenges researchers face is conformation bias. People love data that confirms what they expect and often question results that don't. Facebook's Head of Global Core Ads and Measurement Product Marketing, Jaideep Mukerji, observes, "the more your research is in line with what you were initially thinking, the more people are likely to embrace it and champion it. If something is outside the norm, there are so many ways holes can be poked in the research that it makes it easy for people to discount it." Context is the antidote to this poison.

Sauriol points to an iconic study which brilliantly reveals how what you look for can determine what you see. The 'Gorillas in Our Midst' experiment by psychologists Daniel Simons and Christopher Chabris is a classic.

In the experiment, subjects were asked to watch a short video and to count the basketball passes. It seems a simple request, but it was made more taxing because people had to count basketball passes by the team wearing white shirts, while a black- shirted team also passed a ball. This caused people to focus on a specific endpoint.

While respondents tried to count basketball passes, in the video a person dressed in a gorilla suit walked across the screen. Half the people in the experiment never saw the gorilla, because they were focused on counting the passes.

Teppo Felin, a professor of strategy at Oxford, suggests this experiment illuminates how important ingoing expectations are. He recently wrote, "Imagine you were asked to watch the clip again, but this time without receiving any instructions. After watching the clip, imagine you were then asked to report what you observed. You might report that you saw two teams passing a basketball. You are very likely to have observed the gorilla. But having noticed these things, you are unlikely to have simultaneously recorded any number of other things. The clip features a large number of other obvious things that one could potentially pay attention to and report: the total number of basketball passes, the overall gender or racial composition of the individuals passing the ball, the number of steps taken by the participants. If you are looking for them, many other things are also obvious in the clip: the hair color of the participants, their attire, their emotions, the color of the carpet (beige), the 'S' letters spray-painted in the background, and so forth."

To Sauriol, the 'Gorillas in Our Midst' study perfectly "illustrates the point that you've got to pull your head up sometimes. You've got to look at what's going on around you. You can't be so focused on that one data point."

What you are looking for matters. Looking at a broader context, and keeping an open mind is critical—if you want to notice the gorilla in the room.

Context can make the insights penetrate

Sometimes, combining different types of information can make a finding memorable. Visa was examining why some credit card owners were not using their cards. For some people, it turned out to be about gaining control over their spending. The study had an array of impressive data. But it was a simple video clip of one woman that drove home how important, and challenging, controlling spending was for some consumers.

Sauriol described an in-home interview with a woman who had a credit card, but was using debit exclusively. She was going through a challenging period in her life and needed to regain control of her finances. He asked about her credit card and she said 'yes,' she had one. But to avoid the temptation to use it, she kept in the freezer, in a block of ice. He asked to see it and "she pulled it out. It was literally a block of ice with a card in the middle of it. The two-minute video hammered home every single data point in the presentation about the need for more control. Everyone walked away from that presentation picturing her and her situation. That, to me, is the power of including additional sources of information and context with the data points."

A simple story can be told throughout an organization and will live on in people's memories. A 100-page PowerPoint will be buried on a server somewhere and forgotten—even though, ironically, it might later provide helpful context.

The act of gathering contextual information can also have the benefit of breaking down the silos that hobble organizations. Twitter's Maggie Kishibe said that, historically, Twitter has been relatively siloed. Engineering and product research stuck together, and the insights team worked with marketing, and "never the two shall meet," she says. Her group, in trying to find contextual information on consumers' concerns about privacy, spoke to the product research and advertising research teams. "Hey, do you guys have any information on privacy?" It turns out they did.

This investigation helped build bridges that benefited the whole company. When Kishibe shared her findings with the other teams, those insights spread throughout the organization. They ultimately drew the attention of Twitter CEO Jack Dorsey—who tweeted out the results.

Linking data longitudinally

In addition to synthesizing different pieces of information at a macro level, there is great value in linking other data sets with survey data. They do a lot of that at TD, where they have copious amounts of customer information. TD was, for example, interested in the value of its reputation—its corporate image. By linking survey measures of people's image of the bank with longitudinal data of its value, they saw the direct link between perception and past and future profitability. "It becomes very insightful when you can take claimed information, and match it to actual behavior, and then use that to predict future behavior," says Meghan Nameth.

Shawn Henry runs several communities in New Zealand in which he marries customer data with survey data. One of them is a telecommunications company. "We did a transactional segmentation for them," he explains, "and while we spent three months massaging and cleaning their customer data, we ran a whole bunch of market research on their community: concept testing, ad testing, media awareness, profiling, that kind of stuff. Once the segmentation was done, we uploaded the transactional segments into the community. Then we pulled in all the research we'd been doing for the previous three months. We were able to profile the transactional segments the following week." This segmentation will link to every study going forward as well, adding tremendous value.

Stepping back to see the bigger picture

Mukerji started at Facebook after the Instagram acquisition, and was one of the founding members of the Instagram Marketing Science team. He points to how the accumulation of repeated studies, combined with multiple streams of data and qualitative connections, can reveal profound insights: "We were noticing, over time, that Instagram ads were performing a little differently than Facebook ads. They were both performing well, but Instagram ads tended to work better at some of the upper funnel metrics, like ad recall or brand awareness, whereas the Facebook ones tended to work a little bit better for things like brand favorability or stated purchase intent. So that was a curious question. We had noticed this through hundreds of studies."

"I was able to start looking across what other teams were doing. Some of these teams were using methodologies out of neuroscience. By pulling these different strands of research together, we realized that people spend more time looking at images on an Instagram ad. On Facebook they spend more time looking at the text, and that's a function of how people use those apps."

"On Facebook, people might be more interested in reading text, whereas on Instagram it is much more about the visual experience. The ad unit on Instagram has the image first, followed by the text. On Facebook it is the text first, followed by the image. That's a really obvious thing, but I don't think anyone had ever stopped to think that through."

"These ad units have all the same components, but they are laid out differently. Will that potentially have some impact on how people are perceiving and digesting the ads? It just took someone who could pull it all together."

Not every example of how context adds value needs to be quantitative or longitudinal. Sometimes a historical or semiotic perspective is key.

Coffee in India

Ritanbara Mundrey, Head of Consumer and Customer Insights at Nestlé India, delivered a paper at the ESOMAR Congress that beautifully illustrates what she, in her subtitle, calls "the power of cross pollination." She presented a story about coffee in India. Coffee consumption in that country is extremely low compared to the consumption of tea. Coffee has just 0.003% share of the combined tea and coffee market. But Nescafé has an almost 90% market share in coffee, so they want to grow category consumption. "In a market where in-home coffee consumption is still occasional," she says, "cafés are contesting Nescafé's leadership and redefining coffee for the emerging consumer." The burning question is: "What could Nescafé do to uphold its position as the coffee expert?"

The standard approach would be to run another wave of their usage and attitude tracking, and look at drivers and barriers to consumption. While that would provide a good understanding of the current market, she realized it would not help her learn "how to shake the status quo." She decided to explore three questions: What can be learned from tea consumption in other tea-drinking nations? Why is tea consumption so high in India? and What can be learned from other categories with similar challenges?

They identified the UK and Japan as useful comparators because they were strong tea drinking cultures where coffee consumption had increased. They explored coffee's historical evolution, how it was advertised, and current consumption metrics and trends. What they found is that WWII made all the difference. American soldiers in the UK had coffee in their rations, and that sparked growth in a moribund market. In Japan, the post-war wave of Americanism swept in coffee—along with many other aspects of American life.

They also discovered that coffee had found a way to co-exist with, rather than displace, tea. It was not being sold in a niche. Its usage occasions were diverse: "Morning start, social connections, mid-day recharge."

In seeking to understand why tea was so strong in India, they looked at its history. They were shocked to find that, while India had a long history as a tea exporter, widespread domestic consumption was relatively recent. Fifty years back, tea was considered elitist and expensive. People didn't know how to make it; they thought it was a health hazard, and adoption was slow. That's exactly the image coffee has in India today. What changed everything for tea was widespread advertising and sampling, a decrease in cost, a dispelling of myths, and very strong and specific positioning.

Mundrey sought to learn from the lessons of another category. She picked chocolate. It competes against Indian sweetmeats (mithai) and, like coffee, is led by a dominant brand and has struggled to get much use. In this situation they employed a semiotic approach, decoding mithai's cultural role. They found: "In India, sweetmeats are more than just pleasure. Sweetmeats and their associated occasions range from offerings to Gods at temples, to the symbolic desire and blessing for good times ahead, to communal celebrations like a wedding or a festival. These are far removed from the individual, hedonistic, lustful code of chocolates in the west." Chocolate makers radically changed its positioning by adopting the codes of mithai in its advertising and gained considerable share.

She concludes, "Employing such an approach took us beyond the conventional research outputs of a need state analysis. At the same time, a studied review also avoided the pitfalls of opinion-led decision making, leaving the facts to speak for themselves. It helped us understand how tea and coffee coexist – what are the routes available to coffee. That tea drinking was of recent origin and addressing barriers and growing familiarity were key to consumption. And lastly it highlighted the need for an India-specific, culturally relevant discourse."

A great example of not analyzing in isolation, and thinking outside the survey.

Connect the dots

Let's end this chapter like we started it, with our enigmatic dot.

•

On its own, we don't really know what it is. The lack of context renders it easy to project multiple meanings onto it, perhaps wildly mistaken ones. That can happen with a single piece of research in isolation.

There is power in connecting the dots.

Chapter 4 – Stop Asking Why and Start Making Connections

"People say, 'Consumers lie all the time.' They don't lie. They're just answering the question you asked them."
Pamela Mittoo, Coca-Cola.

"How important is value to you when choosing which brand of paint to purchase?" "Why do you say that?" "When it comes to air travel, which is more important to you: saving money or safety?" These kinds of questions get asked all the time. The answers they elicit are not just useless, they are misleading. They steer us away from the truth and instead provide us with false information that confirms accepted myths.

Questions like "what is important?" and "why do you say that?" get asked because they are easy. They are easy to write, easy to explain to others, and easy to report back. They are seductively simple. But they are poison.

These kinds of questions substitute illusion for truth. And to make matters worse, the picture the answers paint appears plausible. The answers "make sense." That's what makes them so dangerous.

Why is asking 'why' wrong?

Asking 'why?' is problematic because it sits at the overlap of three inconvenient truths. Firstly, we are blind to our motivations. Secondly, our conscious mind creates plausible reasons for our often-unconscious choices. Thirdly, when we provide those reasons, we are deeply influenced by social conventions, and use our answers to get along in the world.

In other words, we don't know why we do what we do, but we are good at making up the answers that we think will satisfy the person we are answering to. The worst part is that we are oblivious to our own ignorance and the inadequacy of our attempts at explanation, because this is the way the world goes 'round.

No wonder it is so easy to ask these kinds of "why" questions. It comes naturally.

What's important?

Let's look at one example of a question that provides misleading information. Here is a typical question about cars, and why people buy them: "I'd like you to think about the last car you purchased. On a scale of 1 to 10 where 10 is very important and 1 not at all important, how important were the following to you when deciding which car to purchase: Gas mileage; Safety record; How sexy the car made you feel."

Twelve hundred car owners answered these questions. We learned that the things that are logically important—like mileage and safety—are both rated as being very important. In fact, they are equally important. They both had an average score of 8/10. What is unimportant is how sexy the car makes you feel. It got an average rating of 4, with 33% of people giving it a 1/10.

People who rated the importance of the car making you feel sexy as less than a 6 were asked, "Why did you say 'how sexy the car made you feel' was not important?" In answering, people often struggled to fathom why we would even ask that.

People wrote things like: "What does it have to do with buying a car? It's a ridiculous and inappropriate question to ask an adult"; "It's not how I look driving it or how others think I look in it. It's safety and mileage that are important to me"; "Really?? You're really asking me that? A car is for transporting."

What is happening here is typical in that people are telling us that the logical answers are important and the seemingly illogical one is unimportant. But if gas mileage is so critical, why does my neighbor—who lives in an apartment and drives a bus for the transit commission—have a giant Ford F-150 pick-up truck? A Honda Civic would get him around the city just fine, and it would give him about 60% more miles per gallon.

People told us that cars are, of course, not about being sexy. But then why is a red sports car a cliché for someone going through a midlife crisis? In fact, why do sports cars even exist if they are not somehow a reflection of who you are or who you want to be?

When we asked people what was important, we got perfectly socially acceptable answers. What we didn't get was an insight into what people really do, and how they really decide. We got misleading information because people are ever ready to give plausible answers to our questions—even if they don't know the answer.

Daniel Gilbert, in his highly readable and often hilarious book *Stumbling on Happiness*, reports, "research suggests that people are *typically unaware* of the reasons they are doing what they are doing, but when asked for a reason they readily supply one. For example, when volunteers watch a computer screen on which words appear for just a few milliseconds, they are unaware of seeing the words and are unable to guess what words they saw. When the word *hostile* is flashed, volunteers judge others negatively. When the word *elderly* is flashed, volunteers walk slowly. When the word *stupid* is flashed, volunteers perform poorly on tests. When these volunteers are later asked to explain why they judged, walked or scored the way they did, two things happen: First, they don't know, and second, they do not say, 'I don't know.' Instead, their brain quickly considers the facts of which they *are* aware ('I walked slowly') and draws the same kinds of plausible but mistaken inferences about themselves that an observer would probably draw about them ('I am tired')."

Ihno Froehling at GSK in Switzerland has seen this in action. He conducted some accompanied shopping research and discovered how little people really can report about what they do, and why. In his research, they videotaped people going through a store, shopping for specific items. They watched where they went, and what they did. Then they debriefed with the shoppers, asking what they did and what they looked at. They asked, "Why did you do this and that? Why did you look at that?"

In addition to videotaping them, they used eye tracking to see where people were looking. Then they sat with the shopper, after the initial debrief, and watched the eye tracking playback. That allowed the shoppers to see where their gaze really went. "We had the recording of the eye tracking, and then we sat in a room next to the store, and we walked the respondents through the recording of this eye tracking. And there you could see that they looked at completely different things than they reported looking at, which they weren't consciously aware of. It was strikingly clear that a lot of the explanations and the whys they gave us were just made up, because we were asking them something they actually couldn't answer." He explained: "When you see the behavior—and even the respondents then saw their own behavior—I think we made much better sense out of it. Because then they're like: 'Oh, I thought I was doing this, but I actually did that.'"

People are reason-giving machines. That has to do with how we think, and how we get along with others.

Think fast!

Psychologist Daniel Kahneman won a Nobel Prize for his work on behavioral economics. Behavioral economics is concerned primarily with how we process information and make decisions. He suggests the brain's operations can be categorized into two systems:

"System 1 operates automatically and quickly, with little or no effort and no sense of voluntary control";

"System 2 allocates attention to the effortful mental activities that demand it, including complex computations."

Another way to think of it is that System 1 is fast, intuitive and emotional, while System 2 is slower, deliberative and logical.

Kahneman suggests that when we think about who we are and the choices we make, we like to believe we are primarily using System 2, "the conscious, reasoning self that has beliefs, makes choices and decides what to think about and what to do."

But hundreds of experiments have confirmed that System 1 thinking is the primary driver of our choices. We tend to make snap judgments and spur-of-the-moment choices, and then rationalize them to ourselves. We believe we are using System 2 thinking because System 1 thinking "effortlessly originates impressions and feelings that are the main sources of the explicit beliefs and deliberate choices of System 2." The notion of System 1 and System 2 thinking is, of course, a metaphor.

British behavioral scientist Nick Chater challenges that metaphor in his provocative new book *The Mind is Flat: The Illusion of Mental Depth and The Improvised Mind.* He sets forth a compelling theory that we have just one way of thinking: we make it up in the moment, based on a sparse combination of perception, context, and memory. He argues, using an impressive review of neuroscience, behavioral psychology, artificial intelligence and perception, that we have no unconscious thoughts—we have only the illusion of depth and solidity.

"Our brains are spectacular engines of improvisation that can, in the moment, generate a color, an object, a memory, a belief or a preference, spin a story or reel off a justification," writes Chater. The brain "is such a compelling storyteller that we are fooled into thinking that it is not inventing our thoughts 'in the moment' at all, but fishing them from some deep inner sea of pre-formed colours, objects, memories, beliefs or preferences, of which our conscious thoughts are merely the shimmering surface. But our mental depths are confabulation—a fiction created in the moment by our own brain."

This, he suggests, explains why so many studies indicate instability in our choices and beliefs, often depending on contextual effects. Writing about how people respond differently to the ways risks are framed he says, "at one moment people shy away from risk; yet at the next moment they embrace it. This makes no sense if we make our choices by referring to some inner oracle, but it makes perfect sense if we are improvising: conjuring up reasons, in the moment, to justify one choice or another."

So, while we like to think of ourselves as rational creatures, we are largely driven by emotional reactions we are not aware of. Neuroscientist V.S. Ramachandran summed this up nicely: "Our mental life is governed mainly by a cauldron of emotions, motives and desires which we are barely conscious of, and what we call our conscious life is usually an elaborate post-hoc rationalization of things we really do for other reasons."

So here we have two of our inconvenient truths: We are blind to our motivations, and our conscious mind creates plausible reasons for our often-unconscious choices. The third truth is that when we provide those reasons we are deeply influenced by social conventions and use our answers to get along in the world.

Social creatures

Life is a lot easier when people are not in conflict. As a result, we have developed a series of habits that tend to reinforce interpersonal harmony. The phenomenon of social mimicry, for example, is well understood—even if it is a little embarrassing when we catch ourselves doing it. People tend to subtly adopt the facial expressions, postures, and ways of speaking of those they are interacting with, and research shows that doing so helps people get along better.

We do a similar kind of thing when we give reasons. We are hugely influenced by who we are "conversing" with—even if the communication is written. Sociologist Charles Tilly in his book *Why?* delves into "what happens when people give reasons…and why." He found that people "often settle for reasons that are superficial, contradictory, dishonest, or—at least from an observer's viewpoint—

farfetched. Whatever else they are doing when they give reasons, people are clearly negotiating their social lives."

Commonly given reasons, according to Tilly, fall into four categories:

1. Convention: "I'm sorry I spilled my coffee; I'm such a klutz."

2. Narratives: "My friend betrayed me because she was jealous of my sister."

3. Technical cause-effect accounts: "A short circuit in the ignition system caused the engine rotors to fail."

4. Codes or workplace jargon: "We can't turn over the records. We're bound by statute 369."

In the world of survey research, we get a lot of conventions— convenient shorthand answers that will be socially acceptable. "The acceptability of such reasons does not depend on their truth," says Tilly, "much less on their explanatory value, but on their appropriateness to the social situation."

Given that we typically don't know why we do what we do, and we are quick to make up reasons that we think are socially acceptable, it is easy to see how asking "why" can provide us with information that is not only unhelpful, it is harmful. Instead of shining a penetrating light on a problem, asking why casts a distorted shadow that masquerades as the answer.

But asking why makes sense

People often have a hard time accepting that asking why is, in the context of insights, a bad idea. It is, after all, a convention we use in our day-to-day lives. Froehling finds that marketers just assume that asking why is appropriate, and are often puzzled when researchers don't do it. "They prefer much more the: 'Let's just get eight mums in the room, and we ask them why?' And then they give us an answer, and then we're fine," he says. "This is what they can better relate to," he explains.

He has found that if he says, "Look, we know now why this is the case," marketers might say, 'Ah, so you asked a consumer, and he told you.' It's like: 'No. I looked at what they say on this topic, and then I saw how they behaved in this situation, and therefore, I can derive why they do things, right?'" He said, "people are interesting, in that they struggle with that."

"I have explained this to clients who are like, 'Ooh…are you not listening? I thought you were the Insights manager. Your job is to respect what consumers say. They are the boss, right?' Then my response is, 'Yes, but I take them so seriously that I listen to them in a way that helps me to better understand,'" he explained. "It includes looking beyond what people say and actually understanding the why."

"I respect the consumer more than to take what he or she tells me at face value," Froehling said. "Or maybe I just made that up to feel better," he said with a sly laugh.

Why is about making connections

So, what do we do, given that asking for reasons is unhelpful? Should we shelve this whole survey research thing and just observe people? That is part of the answer, but it is not the whole answer.

"It is widely accepted that people are poor witnesses to their own motivations," says Ray Poynter, "which is why there has been a growth in the interest in behavioral economics, observational data, and non-conscious measurements." He points the way to some very useful streams of data to help us understand what is important. But to get to why we need to start making connections.

"Why?" is revealed when we ask about perceptions of a politician, for example, and connect that to whom people voted for. Or when an ethnographer observes the relationship between a person's behavior and their context. Or when we measure whether there is a relationship between seeing McDonald's as "fun" or "disgusting," and how often people eat there.

Getting to why is about making connections and seeing what influences what. In the world of insights that might mean mining databases, connecting survey data to customer records, or correlating two variables within a survey. In all those cases, making connections allows us to avoid the error of asking "why?"

That leads us to the importance of learning as a journey.

Chapter 5 – Stop Trying to Learn Everything at Once and Start Being Agile and Iterative

"An organization's ability to learn, and translate that learning into action rapidly, is the ultimate competitive advantage."
Jack Welch, former chairman and CEO of General Electric

In 1496, Henry VII sponsored John Cabot to "go and find the new land." In his first voyage, "he went with one ship, his crew confused him, he was short of supplies and ran into bad weather, and he decided to turn back," according to a letter written by a Bristol merchant. His second voyage, a year later, saw him depart with supplies for "seven or eight months." He left Bristol May 2, 1497, and returned August 6, having landed briefly at Cape Bonavista, Newfoundland, before returning.

Today, my boss commutes between London and Toronto. The flight from Toronto to London is seven hours. Times change.

Research used to be about long surveys that took months to execute. Now, research can be executed overnight and absorbed and acted on the next day. This makes it possible to use an agile and iterative approach in which you learn, adjust, test, refine, and pivot or dig deeper as you accumulate knowledge.

Research has sped up because the world is moving faster and faster, powered by ever-changing technology and a transformation of culture. We live in a time of instant messaging, six-second ads and 280-character tweets. The speed of business has increased. There is a need for constant innovation and relentless improvement.

Business demands nimble responses. Insights can't come back in four to six months. Agile and iterative research lets you move quickly.

Getting to know you

Imagine you wanted to get to know someone. Here's one approach: ask the person questions for 30 minutes, go away and puzzle over the answers, and then never see that person again. Here's another approach: You start up a conversation, hear what they say, and then reply. And then you keep talking, back and forth. Which strategy is most likely to help you get to know that person?

That may seem a silly question, but it underscores the reality that an agile and iterative approach to research is far better than the typical one-off survey. An ongoing dialogue is more efficient and effective. It is more efficient because you end up only asking questions that are relevant. It is more effective because you learn as you go, adjusting as knowledge accumulates.

The need for speed

Twitter is a fast-growing, quickly evolving company. Its approach to insights can't afford to be mired in old, slow ways of doing research. The exploration would be irrelevant before it was complete. Twitter's Maggie Kishibe is keenly attuned to how different that model is because she came to Twitter after years spent doing research for consumer packaged goods companies, which are not known for their nimbleness. She now struggles to work with "traditional" research companies because they can't keep up with the needs of the business. She needs agile research.

"I come from working with Unilever, Nestlé, and Loblaws," she explains, "and they do massive projects that take months and months. And then, I went to San Francisco, and I'm working with Intel and Dell and innovative tech companies, and they just want snippets. Every week, there's a different study you're reporting on."

She has found that if she doesn't move quickly, her stakeholders lose interest, because the business has moved on. She explains that "one of the challenges that I've had is working with a more traditional vendor on a project. The project had great momentum at the beginning. But that momentum has been completely lost because we won't have results for two months." What the team needs is: "Here's what we learned this week; next week we'll have something else. You have to do it that way, rather than 'here's a 50-page report about this big study that we did.'"

An iterative approach allows her to learn as she goes. "After the first study you learn something that adjusts the second, adjusts the third and so on. It's the agile approach." "It's too risky to have these big projects where I'm going to commit to something on month one, but it may be out of date in month four," she explains. "And then, when you go to present it, they say, 'Well, did you ask about this?' and inevitably, the answer is 'no.' Because I didn't have the opportunity to say, 'Let's rethink how we're going to ask this next set of questions.'"

Telstra's Elizabeth Moore finds that "the business expectation around speed has changed." Telstra is now better able to mine customer data and get accurate, up-to-date information almost instantly. That, she says, "puts pressure on other research to be significantly faster."

Telstra has dropped its traditional market share tracking study and is using customer data to impute share. "Instead of waiting eight weeks, and having measures of error you could drive a truck through—and spending over a million dollars a year on it—we now know, in a week, what the shift in market share is."

That's a much more agile way of obtaining insights. And with the money they saved from switching the tracker to an analysis of customer data, Moore says they now dig into questions like: "Why have people left us? What were the main reasons that they're leaving us? Where have they gone? Why have they chosen that?" That's a much better use of time and budget.

A journey of learning

Twitter's Kishibe mentioned the agile approach, adapting as you go. Coca-Cola's Pamela Mittoo sees the value of an agile approach too. She thinks of learning as a journey. She knows her destination, but she is comfortable not knowing exactly how she will get there. Mittoo says, "If I know my destination is 20 miles down the road—and I could go many different ways—I just need to get to the five-mile marker first. I know that's a waypoint where I'm going to gather some learnings," before deciding where to explore next.

Mittoo works in the innovation team at Coca-Cola and does a lot of product development. She finds a nimble approach is essential. She describes how an iterative process allows her to pivot as she learns. She might say to a consumer, "'Hey, here's a high-level idea. Would you like a sparkling beverage with paprika in it?' and they say, 'Yeah, that sounds great.' And then, you start making some prototypes. 'Well, when would you use it?' 'I wouldn't replace my Coca-Cola with it. But you know what? When I was young, my grandmother gave me paprika to cool down, if I was running all the time.' 'Hmm. Maybe this is not a sparkling initiative. Maybe this is a sports drink initiative?'"

Maz Amirahmadi, CEO of ABN Impact in Singapore, also appreciates the flexibility of an agile and iterative approach, in that you can not only follow up on ideas, but you can also be flexible in the methodology you use, switching between quantitative and qualitative approaches as appropriate. He says, "if we get a response that we weren't expecting, we can pivot and dig into the question," qualitatively. Using an agile approach, he can stop and ask, "I wonder why that is? Now we can put those questions in a discussion forum.

Previously, we'd say, 'Hmm, I wonder why that is?' And that would be the end of it."

The ability to pivot, based on what people tell you, opens the door to voyages of discovery that are simply impossible with one-off surveys. It also has the benefit of keeping marketers focused on the consumer.

Pfizer Consumer Health has, historically, done large consumer segmentations that they revisit every few years. But those days are past, according to Seth Minsk, Director of Consumer Insights. He sees benefits for marketers in a more agile approach because consumers become more top of mind and accessible. "If you get used to shorter, more frequent interactions with consumers, it means you're thinking about the consumer more often. And you're not thinking of the consumer as a doorstop that's been sitting on your desk for two years. You bring the consumer to life in a much more compelling manner."

An ongoing conversation

Agile learning journeys are most effective when they are based in a community—a group of well-profiled people that you can return to on an ongoing basis. They can be just a few thousand people and focused on one product or category. Or they can be vast and representative of the general population, like our Springboard America and Maru Voice Canada communities. One important benefit is that you know a great deal about these people and can use that information to enrich your analysis and avoid asking unnecessary questions.

Shawn Henry of Camorra Research in New Zealand was an early pioneer in community-based research. He says, "The community approach has been a revelation, in terms of the relationship with the respondent. You can do quant; you can do online qualitative; you can invite them to focus groups. And the whole time you're carrying around a cumulative knowledge of what they think, and who they are. That is a stark change from the traditional 80's CATI research, where everything is anonymous." It is also very different from interacting with unknown respondents who get routed to your survey from a sample exchange.

In a community, you and the members are on a journey together. They know where your questions are coming from, and where they are going. Respondents love the interactive dialogue because they see their voice is heard, and their input makes a difference.

Peter Harris, former President of the Australian Market and Social Research Society, explains how valuable that is. He told me about software user experience research where he was "talking to people on a Monday, fixing the software on the Tuesday, talking to the same people on Wednesday, fixing it again on Thursday, getting it out Friday. You talk to the same people, over time, who already understand what you're trying to do. They know you fixed something. They're ready to move on to the next thing."

The right questions for the right people

Paul Holtzman, Senior Vice President Data Science at Vision Critical, has found that an iterative and agile approach also has the benefit of allowing you to tailor questionnaires and analysis based on how people responded to previous questions. He describes an initial study in which "bump hunting" was used to segment people based on their responses to some foundational questions. "I learned there were six chunks, six clusters of people based on the information I had in hand." Based on that, he crafted a second study that was customized for each of the segments.

"That second survey really needed to be modularized. I was sending it to six different chunks of people with different questions." This responsiveness allows researchers to test different materials with each segment. "Each of those six groups that I had identified had a different stimulation that would be most effective. Each had a different optimization plan." Or, as he says, "you can even make the decision, I've got six segments here; I only want to pursue two."

An agile and iterative approach to research allows you to do research at the speed of the business, lets you pivot and dig deeper as you move forward, enables you to build layer upon layer of learning, and permits you to ask the right questions of the right people. It is a much superior model to viewing every survey in isolation.

The agile thrive

In the early days of research, surveys tended to be long because interviewing was expensive. You had to collect all the information you needed in one survey because you were not going to reconnect with the respondent.

Today, using a community allows you to conduct research as an ongoing dialogue. Surveys can be short and focused. Everything you discover builds on previous learnings.

This agile and iterative approach not only provides greater insights, but it is also much more enjoyable for the person completing the survey. This is critically important because, as we'll see in the following chapters, how people feel about your survey will make or break the quality of the information you obtain.

Chapter 6 – Stop Treating Respondents Like a Commodity and Start Treating Them Like People

Who and how you sample can literally kill a business. In 1936, *Literary Digest*, a very popular magazine at the time, conducted a poll on the presidential election. They had done this for every election since 1916 and always correctly predicted the outcome. In 1936 they confidently declared—based on a sample of almost 2.5 million people—that the Republican candidate, Governor Alfred Landon of Kansas, was going to be the next President. But they based their sample on mail-in surveys from their subscribers, automobile registration lists and telephone directories. These sources tended to skew to more affluent people, who tended to vote Republican. At the same time, George Gallup, who used face-to-face interviews and quota sampling, correctly predicted that Franklin Delano Roosevelt would become the 32nd President of the United States.

Gallup went on to become a household name. *Literary Digest*, discredited by their very public mistake, withered and folded soon afterward. The insights industry is repeating that potentially fatal mistake. Many surveys today are being conducted with sample that is unrepresentative and unreliable. The difference between *Literary Digest's* error and current industry practices is that we are at risk of killing the whole industry, not just a single company.

Let's see where the risk is so that we can avoid that fate.

It's convenient

Real probability sampling became extinct many, many years ago, largely before market research really took off. As an industry we've struggled along with various attempts to provide representative—or at least reproducible—samples. Adapting to the times, we have used face-to-face interviews, mail surveys, phone surveys and online surveys, all of which have their biases.

As society has changed, response rates have declined, and the best way to reach representative samples has been transformed by how technology mediates our lives. In the past few years, the industry has discovered new ways to source respondents that magically both reduce costs and increase our ability to find "sample" that will fill our difficult quotas. But, as we will see, this low-price sample has other costs.

Political poll aggregators like Nate Silver and his 538.com website provide useful reality checks on the quality of select sample sources. They have a "pollster rating" program where they compare the results of surveys to actual election results. They grade each pollster on accuracy and bias. While the often-poor ratings of these polls are sobering, they probably represent a relatively rosy picture of the state of the industry. Few companies want to publicize results using their truly dodgy sample.

Does the label match what's in the package?

The world of on-line sample has a bewildering myriad of players. There are agencies, suppliers, sample validators, brokers, and trade desks. They buy, sell, swap, validate, resell and repackage on-line sample. But does the name on the package match the contents? If you are buying sample from company X, is it really from them or is it coming from somewhere else?

"Those that respect the law and love sausage should watch neither being made," wrote Mark Twain. One might be tempted to say the same about sample. It's complicated, and sometimes you just don't want to know exactly how you got it.

But we can't afford to turn a blind eye to sample quality when it determines the reliability and reproducibility of our research. If our sample is bad, the conclusions we draw from our research will mislead those who need our insights.

A few years back there was a scandal in Europe when it was discovered that some of what was being sold as beef was actually horsemeat. "Horsegate" involved some of the biggest brands on the continent. CBC News reported at the time, "More than a dozen nations have detected horse flesh in processed products such as factory-made burger patties, lasagnas, meat pies and meat-filled pastas. The investigations have been complicated by elaborate supply chains involving multiple cross-border middlemen."

Investigations revealed that correctly-labeled horsemeat was sold from two Romanian abattoirs to a Dutch meat trader, who sold it on to a Cypriot company that, in turn, sold it to a French firm who sold it on to a company in Luxembourg. Somewhere along the way, the horsemeat was relabeled "beef." When it finally reached food manufacturers, it ended up in foods sold by such industry giants as Nestlé, Ikea, Tesco and Asda.

Insert "sample" for "processed food products" in the following report on the horsemeat scandal and see if it sounds familiar:

"Processed food products — a business segment with traditionally low margins that often leads producers to hunt for the cheapest suppliers — often contain ingredients from multiple suppliers in different countries, who themselves at times subcontract production to others, making it hard to monitor every link in the production chain."

Research by Millward Brown's Compete, as well as research by companies that route sample, has traced the original sources of sample purchased from many leading agencies, brokers and exchanges. In many cases, it turns out the sample originated elsewhere, typically from a river sample supplier, who in turn is aggregating sample from many sources.

The name river sample evokes visions of pristine waters flowing gently, with babbling rapids and a meandering path through a verdant forest. But the reality of river sample is very different. It is actually a muddy swamp of respondents who are coming from "get paid to do surveys" sites or from social media, or publisher sites promising them something if they do a survey. This sets up an unfortunate dynamic with respondents. They are in it for the money, and the pittance they are offered makes it clear how little we value them. It's not surprising that this would affect the data.

Our research, as well as The Advertising Research Foundation's Foundations of Quality 2 study (ARF FOQ 2) and others, has shown that river sample has problems with reliability and reproducibility. Using a confidence interval of 95%, one would expect to see differences between two waves of a study of 5% or so. With river sample we typically see variations that are double or triple that. Is research using these sample sources scientific, or more akin to tea leaf reading?

Wine, cheese and scotch—it's all about the source

Another common source of sample is communities or panels. They are made up of people who have joined with the intention of doing surveys. They know that they are a part of a group and expect to receive invitations. These are more reliable sources than river sample, but a critical question is where do the people come from?

The source can make quite a difference. We only need to think about the examples of wine, cheese, and scotch to understand this.

Sparkling white wine is made all over the world, but the only sparkling white wine that can be called Champagne is from the Champagne region of France.

Under Italian law, "Parmigiano-Reggiano" is the name for cheese produced only in the provinces of Parma, Reggio Emilia, Bologna, Modena, and Mantua. European law classifies the name, as well as the translation "Parmesan," as a protected designation of origin.

On the island of Islay in Scotland, the last time I was there, the water was so filled with peat that it ran red as I drew a bath for the kids. The peat bog source of the water is what drives the strong peaty flavor of Islay scotches like Laphroaig, Ardbeg and Lagavulin.

In all these places, the source is so important to the flavor that laws exist to ensure consumers get the real thing. In research, the source is equally important for sample.

A common source for large communities or panels that are designed to be representative of the population is loyalty cards and retailers' credit cards. They are attractive to companies that are building or maintaining a community because they are a quick way to get access to a lot of people, and those people tend to be more compliant. They are also relatively inexpensive sources of recruitment. That sounds like a good deal, but there is a catch. The sources tend to flavor the results, in ways that aren't so tasty.

Some of the effects are predictable. For example, if you had people recruited from a loyalty card you would expect the incidence of shopping at stores that accept that particular loyalty card to be higher than usual. But that can have knock-on effects as to what brands they buy, based on which products these stores carry or promote. Likewise, a test of a coupon-based promotion is likely to overestimate interest, because people who use loyalty cards tend to be more attracted to coupons. And there can be all sorts of other effects that might not be so straightforward. These effects were revealed rather spectacularly in a study which tracked loyalty card ownership and a variety of other variables.

One of the Canadian panels we track—we'll call it panel A—apparently switched sources. In year one of our tracking, 52% of the people from that panel had an HBC loyalty card. The next year that had decreased to 40%. At the same time, the number of people on that panel with a Petro Points card jumped from 58% in year one to 72% in year two. That looks like a switch in recruitment sources. The effect was significant.

When we compared the survey results between year one and year two, they were significantly different on 38% of the items we tracked. Did the world change that much? No. What changed was the source from which the panel was recruited.

This influence of sources that skews results is exactly what sank the *Literary Digest*. Unfortunately, Panel A is commonly used by many of world's largest companies. What does that mean for a business that is making decisions based on research using that sample?

Coercion corrodes quality

Another popular source of sample is people who are seeking access to content, like an article or a video. What typically happens is that you are doing an online search, find content you want to read, and just when you are ready to download it, you are stopped and asked to answer a few questions before you get access.

That can seem like a reasonable bargain; you ask a person to answer a short survey and they get what they want. But what does it do to the person you've asked to do the survey? Will they be delighted to answer your questions? Or will they see it as an irritating exercise that is separating them from the object of their desire?

We've been testing the validity and reliability of a very well-known company that offers surveys with sample from publisher sources. For our test, we looked at usage of different types of social media, including Facebook and Twitter. The survey asked people which social media platforms they use. We started tracking this in 2014, including multiple waves in the first year.

These data suggest social media usage grew quickly in 2014, peaked early in 2015 and started into a steep decline in 2016, before falling back to 2014 levels in 2017. Facebook, according to this sample source, was used by 39% of the U.S. online population in April 2014. By November 2014 usage had apparently exploded up to 54%. In January 2015 it had risen further to 59%. Then things allegedly went off the rails for Facebook. In January 2016 usage had plummeted to 47%. By February 2017 it had dropped down to 39%, and in February 2018 it was 38%—basically back where we started in 2014.

The other social media we tracked showed similar roller coaster rides of increase and decrease in usage. That would be uncomfortable news to a lot of investors, and would probably surprise a lot of people who are using these services. But does this sample source reflect reality? Apparently not.

The Pew Research Center—which is meticulous about its sampling— has been tracking social media use among internet users for a few years, giving us a reliable check for these numbers. The center's data paint a very different picture. Not only do they show consistent slow growth in usage, but the numbers are much higher. For example, our publisher sample put Facebook usage at 47% and declining in 2016. At the same time, Pew saw usage grow to 79%. That is such an enormous gap, and with such a different pattern, it is clear that the publisher sample is completely misleading.

There are many reasons why the data from the publisher sample source could be so wrong. They could be sampling an unrepresentative set of people. The data could be weighted incorrectly because imputation methods are used to estimate the demographics. It could also be that the people answering the questions just don't care about the survey, so they don't bother to answer correctly.

Ultimately, it is probably a combination of all those errors. The data could be wrong because the sample might be unrepresentative. The risk of that is high if all respondents came from a single source—like people trying to get access to a piece of content called, for example, "I Hate Social Media." But the provider says it sources each project from a mixture of publishers, and it balances the sample to be representative of the U.S. population.

The fact that the demographics are estimated rather than being measured directly is problematic, and certainly there are errors. But when we looked at the data weighted and unweighted, the differences were not large—definitely not large enough to account for the kind of variation we observed.

The high cost of cheap sample

How did we get here? How did poor quality sample become so commonplace? Paradoxically, it is because research has become exponentially cheaper and faster over the past decades. That has created expectations that have led the industry to a dangerous place.

Back when Gallup used face-to-face interviews, research was slow and expensive. It could take months to plan a sample frame, send people door to door, and interview hundreds or thousands of people in their homes. The cost of an in-home face-to-face survey is around $120 or more. A telephone interview cost would be around one-tenth of that. And when I was involved in telephone-based research, studies would often take weeks to complete. Yesterday I conducted a study using Google Consumer Surveys—a popular publisher-based sample source—for 12 cents a completed survey. It was done fielding in a day. That's cheap and fast, for sure. But is the data any good?

While the cost of most things has been slowly rising, the cost of online sample has been declining. That has created the expectation that sample should be inexpensive. Procurement departments don't know anything about sample quality, nor is that their business. Their job is to drive costs down. But when cheaper means lower quality, cost cutting can slice too deep.

The knowledge that research can be turned around quickly has also put a great deal of pressure on researchers to cut corners to get a job done. A researcher who participated in a focus group for the ARF FOQ 2 study exemplified how the pressure can lead people to take short cuts. Reporting on the focus group, ARF said, "Another participant mentioned that at the end of the day, when she needs to find the last few respondents to finish the study, she will turn a blind eye and tell the sample provider to just finish the job and find them. 'I hide my eyes, close my mouth—get me those 50 people, and I don't care how you do it.'"

Changing the channel on poor sample quality

The insights industry has brought itself to the point of crisis by being seduced by the siren call of lower sample costs and quick ways to fill quotas. Cheap and widely used sample sources—like river and publisher—can produce results that are unreliable, if not wildly wrong. How long can this go on before the damage is crippling?

The *Literary Digest* got away with using biased sample for 20 years before they ruined their reputation and lost their business. Using less than reliable sample is like Russian Roulette. You might get away with it for a while, but a day of reckoning is sure to come. We need to put the gun down now.

A great place to start is to do what insights professionals do best: ask smart questions, analyze the answers, and then share what we have learned.

Asking about the source of the sample is crucial. If you ask that about river sample, the answer usually is that it "comes from a blend of many sources." If we picked up a package of food and the ingredient list said, "a blend of many things," we'd probably put it back on the shelf very quickly.

It's important to press for specific answers and concrete data on sources. The truth is that any quality sample has a supplier identification variable attached to it. It doesn't show up in your tables, and it might even be left out of the data set sent to you, but the data is there; you just have to ask for it. If your supplier can't tell you—because they got it from another supplier, who can't trace it either—then we are looking at the kind of situation that allowed Horsegate to happen. Understanding who supplies the sample is a good first step, but it is essential to peel back another layer of this onion.

The next level of questioning is where and how the people are recruited. Watch for many panelists being recruited from a single source, like a loyalty card. Look out too for many members coming from just a handful of sources. Even if they don't have the obvious bias a loyalty card-based sample does, the methods of recruitment might introduce an unknown set of problems. If, for example, 20% of a supplier's people were recruited from a (fictional) site called "Surveys for Fun!" it might be that Surveys for Fun! has discovered that the best way to get to a hard-to-find group like young men is to advertise exclusively on gamer sites. That would skew things in a way that might not be immediately obvious but could distort results later.

It is possible to measure how much each recruiter contributes to your sample. Maru/Blue, for example, includes the source of the recruit in every dataset. That's how they track the quality of that source. It enables them to identify drop-out and response rates for each supplier and thus recognize which are good sources and which are not. You should be able to ask for the recruitment sources for any study you have recently conducted. If they all come from places like "Make Cash Fast," you might want to think twice about using that source again.

A challenge in obtaining good sample is convincing the business the lowest cost option is not necessarily the best. Sample, while important, is far from sexy. Making sure you have good sample is like being a microbiologist conducting quality control at a sausage factory. Do it right and no one cares. Do it wrong and there can be big trouble.

The challenge is getting people to understand and care about sample quality. That's why I started this chapter with the *Literary Digest* case study. It is a powerful example of how bias in a sample source can have disastrous results. The social media debacle with the publisher sample cited earlier is also potent contemporary evidence of just how wrong data can be. And the results of inquiries into sample sources can reveal how easy it is for sample to be unrepresentative or unreliable.

The representativeness of the people who complete your studies makes or breaks the value and validity of your insights. Yet the industry has largely ignored the issue and persisted in using a great deal of sample that is unrepresentative and unreliable. The example of *Literary Digest* and the poll that killed their business should haunt us every time we are tempted to say, "get me those . . . people, and I don't care how you do it."

Insights professionals collectively need to treat respondents as people, and ensure that we engage and encourage them to participate. And when we get them into our survey, we need to treat them well.

Chapter 7 – Stop Conducting Abusive Surveys and Start Putting People First

The job of the insights function is to listen to the voice of the people and solve business problems based on what we have heard. Since our task is connecting with consumers, we must be hyperconscious of their wants and needs. We must "connect" with them. But do the research methods we use reflect that?

Sadly, many of the common practices in research suggest we act as if we are tone-deaf to the consumer and citizen. We know that no one likes long surveys, filled with difficult-to-answer questions that are only of interest to a brand manager—yet we persist in doing them.

Do we really expect the most revealing insights to come from that kind of conversation? What magical thinking makes us believe that ignoring what people want will somehow reveal what they need?

This point of contact with people seems so simple, yet it is really our Achilles' heel. We need to put the respondent first, and stop doing abusive surveys.

A relationship, just not a good one

"Beat them up, get your data and walk away." That's how Patrick Comer of Lucid characterizes much of the research done today. The prioritization of our needs, at the expense of the people who answer our surveys, is not only contrary to our claim to be the voice of the consumer, it undermines the very thing we are setting out to do: reveal what the people think.

"We're continuing to field 30-, 35-, 40-minute long surveys, very complex grid designs, very laborious, and we're not making it fun" Lisa Wilding-Brown, Chief Research Officer at Innovate MR, explains. "If it's not fun for you to take—and you're a researcher—why do you think the average consumer is going to think it's interesting?"

Mendy Orimland, SVP of Revenue at Prodege, joined the world of market research a few years back after working in various other technology-related businesses. He was surprised and dismayed when he discovered how survey takers were typically treated. "It seemed that little thought was given to the fact that there was actually a person at the other end taking the survey. And that was an unspoken thing. Yes, from time to time, somebody got up at a market research conference, and uttered words like: 'The experience needs to be better.' But the issue didn't seem to get much attention or action. In my view, many in the research industry still don't fully respect the time commitment and effort of the respondent, the person actually taking the survey. To me, this is a broken link because, at the end of the day, these are the people giving you all the insights. And we should treat them the same way we'd like to be treated."

Respondents are the source of our understandings. "Treat your respondents for what they are; they are your entire business, mate," says Shawn Henry, Director of Camorra Research. "We are getting paid for our respondents' thoughts and repackaging them. It's not our insights that we are selling. It's the insights derived from our respondents, our participants, who have given up their time and their views."

Bad experiences beget low response rates

The way we treat the people who do our surveys has led to steadily declining response rates. It is becoming harder to recruit people because they have had bad experiences in the past. Annie Pettit, research consultant and author, wrote in an email interview, ". . . response rates—and data quality—have plummeted because researchers failed to respect the human being. . . . Our failure to design high-quality data collection tools has eroded response rates."

That's a problem for us: if the average person doesn't want to do our surveys, how good are the "insights" we get from those who are willing to put up with punishing experiences?

Wilding-Brown provides a powerfully instructive analogy: "Respondents are the polar ice caps of Market Research. We know they are important, but we aren't doing much to reverse the damage of our daily abuse. Of course, we talk a lot about the impact of long surveys, shrinking incentive budgets, hostage-taking routers, and price compression. However, at the end of the day, nothing is changing."

"That, to me, is the frustration point," Wilding-Brown says. "We expect consumers to do everything for us, and yet we are unwilling to make any change or to be even competitive within the environment that we're operating in. It's very problematic, in my mind."

Stop treating people like clinical subjects

What you name things says a lot about your perspective and your approach. We generally call the people who do our surveys "sample." That's a term that generates distance and lets us forget that our surveys are answered by living, breathing, people with demands other than our information needs.

Sample is defined as "a finite part of a statistical population whose properties are studied to gain information about the whole." That's a pretty clinical definition, but it is consistent with how the industry uses the term. We think of sample as a commodity—something you buy more of when you have high drop-out rates or a greater than expected number of disqualifications. But are the people who do our surveys simply "a finite part of a statistical population"?

Sometimes we use a friendlier term: respondents. A respondent is defined as a "person who answers a request for information." I like this definition because it acknowledges the fact that we are talking about people. But it is still very much a research-centric phrase. It is about people doing something for us. I'd propose that there is value in thinking very differently about this. If we call respondents something else, we might change the way we approach them. Let's call them people.

When you think of people, you think of friends and family, neighbors and colleagues. It's harder to justify writing and fielding a study in which most will be disqualified if you think of the respondents as people. Would you want to ask your neighbors to be part of that study?

It's more difficult to ask people to answer a long survey if you think about what your mother would say if you asked her to do it. Likewise, if you think about what your friends would say if you asked them to fill out a mobile-unfriendly grid with seven brands and 32 attributes, you'd be less likely to make that ask. It's much easier to do bad surveys when you're just getting "sample."

Now that I think about it...

Focus groups have been a mainstay of qualitative research since the 1940s. Millions of evenings have been spent in darkened rooms, viewing "the average consumer" sitting around a boardroom table, while the researchers lounge behind a one-way mirror, nibbling on lukewarm catered food and crunching M&Ms. If you are behind the glass, it seems reasonable enough. But what if you are on the other side?

What is the experience of the people who come out? Firstly, they need to be willing to give up a couple of hours of their time, for a modest amount of money. Then we ask them to come to an office building, into a boardroom setting. While that might be an everyday environment for insights professionals, it's not how the majority live and work. And then there is the one-way mirror.

Ever seen people comb their hair, check their teeth, adjust themselves, or put on makeup while standing about a foot away from you? I have, too many times. They think they are looking at a mirror, and you're on the other side, watching them. It's a little weird. But when you think about it, it's extremely weird.

Maz Amirahmadi of ABN Impact in Singapore brought the oddity of this to my attention when we were talking about the respondent experience. He said, "If you started all over again, and you thought, 'Okay, I really need to understand my customers,' you would never come up with the concept of a focus group, where you'd say, 'Okay, let's invite this group of six strangers, and we'll hide behind a mirror and listen to them. And we'll pretend we're not there.' And then somebody turns on a light, and we go, 'Oh, shhh, turn off the light.' This is insane, you know?"

This is an environment where people are treated like subjects, not everyday people. It creates an odd and detrimental dynamic. "Imagine the proposition:" Amirahmadi said, "'Hey, I'd really like to know everything about your life, but I'll tell you what, I'm not going to tell you who I am.'"

Why would people not find that experience weird? Even if they really wanted to come out and share their thoughts, we are asking citizens and consumers to allow themselves to be treated as lab rats, rather than people. No wonder we have problems with professional respondents coming to focus groups. Why would a normal person want that experience?

As an industry, we've assumed a lot of odd habits, and then become oblivious to them. Treating people like lab subjects is one of them. As Amirahmadi says, "for some reason, we think that in a market research environment, we should be careful not to be human."

Long is too long

A common complaint is that surveys are too long. Long surveys lead to poor quality information. As one person told us in a video interview, "When surveys drag on too long, then you lose interest and don't give the answers that really mean something."

Do you hear the alarm bells? We count on people providing answers that "really mean something."

When survey research began, interviews were face-to-face, and long surveys were common—because it was expensive and slow to send someone out to do an in-person interview. Companies took advantage of the opportunity and crammed in every question they could. Besides, they didn't know anything about the people they were talking to, so they started from scratch with each interview. Also, having a face-to-face interviewer present meant there was someone whose job it was to keep people engaged.

This approach conditioned researchers to think that a long survey was both desirable and reasonable. And it led to a thirst for as much data from a single survey as possible. Wilding-Brown calls this approach "gluttonous" and points out that it's selfish and ignores the reality of today's time-challenged world. She suggests it is common for researchers to think, "'I want to ask all the questions I can think of in one session, so it makes it nice and neat and clean for me, as a person who analyzes you.' But that's not how consumers operate, and they're not willing to give you that time and that devotion that they may have done 15, 20 years ago, because they didn't have all of the chaos and the distraction that is the online world that we all operate in today."

Seth Minsk of Pfizer says generational changes mean long surveys are dead. "There's no way that a millennial is sitting at a computer to answer complicated grid questions for 45 minutes. It's not culturally part of their experience."

As surveys get longer, the response rates decrease and the number of drop-outs soars. This leads to unrepresentative sample. And the longer a survey is, the worse the data quality becomes, especially toward the end of the survey. By then, people are bored and just want to get it over with. Yet researchers persist in doing these long studies. Why?

One thing that fuels a drive toward length is project-based budgeting that is designed to fund one-off studies rather than agile learning streams. Another factor is being in the role of an order taker.

One problem with being in the order taker role is a power imbalance, coupled with the order giver's lack of understanding of the implications of their requests. "My business partners don't think about this kind of thing," says Visa's Kristopher Sauriol. "They just think, 'I've got 1,000,001 questions and I want to have them all asked.' They are not thinking about respondent fatigue and dropout rates and data quality issues. They just think it's all going to come back just fine." Intel's Antony Barton echoes that sentiment, saying, "Yeah, it is often the stakeholder who is pushing us to ask all these questions, and if we don't go 'well, after 15 minutes, the quality is going to go down', and if we are not strong enough to push back, it is our own problem."

Another way the order-taker approach can lead to long surveys is poor conceptualization of the objectives and a kitchen sink mentality. Sauriol has found that overly long surveys can be avoided by "being as precise as possible with the objective and the research questions. And the research questions should all ladder back to addressing those objectives. It's about trying to narrow it down as much as possible. 'What do we essentially need to know here?' 'What is critical to our business?' And then focusing on that."

Alternatively, he proposes, "maybe the research question is not necessarily something we do with just one study. Maybe it's something that we take a multipronged approach to, breaking it up into smaller bite-size pieces that allow us more time to really be thorough. If we can break it apart, or we can do a couple of different surveys, that can really allow us to get better data in the end."

Stop disqualifying everyone

When market researchers first conducted surveys, they tried to find people by chance. They knew nothing about them. Surveyors simply knocked on a random door and tried to learn everything about a person that they might need to contextualize the person's answers. To do so, they had to ask about anything that might be relevant. Age? Needed to be asked. Education? Ditto. What about work, voting history, past purchase behaviors, and media habits? They all had to be inquired about in each survey because everyone was an unknown quantity. The interviewer and respondent had never met before, and never would meet again. Researchers and the people they interviewed were just strangers in the night. This need not happen today. But it does, all the time. And people don't like it.

We did some video interviews and asked people what they liked and disliked about doing surveys. Being disqualified after many screening questions was a common complaint. "I wish surveys would be smarter and not ask me the same questions over and over again. That repetitive clicking of how old I am, where I live, what my demographic is, how much money I make. It's kind of a nuisance," one person told us.

A time-pressed young mother, whose baby could be seen in a high chair behind her while she did the interview, said, "The one thing that really bugs me about surveys is when I get a few minutes into them—five or ten minutes—and then it tells me I don't qualify. I just feel like it's a huge waste of my time…. You get halfway through and then it cuts out, and they say they 'met their quota.' It just seems like they don't value my time."

Wilding-Brown suggests 9 out of 10 people who are being routed through sample exchanges fail to qualify for a survey they are screened for. So they get asked to qualify for another study—and get asked basics like age, gender, race and region over and over again. Being disqualified is a terrible respondent experience. I know, because it happened to me.

I recently joined a community offered by an edgy alternative media outlet. I like their content and thought it would be fun to learn more. In joining, I was immediately asked a bunch of demographic questions. No sooner had I completed their profiling questionnaire than I was booted to a router where I was again asked a bunch of the same demographic questions.

Then I was asked a series of improbable questions which included, "Did you personally design your company's logo?" and "Have you personally identified a potential acquisition target that your company bought?" and "Do you currently use any left-handed computer peripherals?" Having none of these qualities, I wasn't eligible to do a survey. I was then routed to another company's set of improbable questions.

I was again asked my gender, my age and my race, before heading on to another set of qualifying questions. I again failed to qualify because I had not sky-dived in the past three months, did not own a turtle, and had not installed an automated sprinkler system in the past six months. What made it all the worse was that none of these studies had anything to do with the media outlet that got me to join their community. It was frustrating, and I quit—even though I was still curious about the turtle study.

It seemed natural to wonder—like the person who wanted surveys to be smarter—why did my profiling information not follow me? Why did I have to be asked the same question over and over again? Why was the system so dumb? The answer is simple. I was not really a member of a community. I was not a known person. I was simply a piece of anonymous "sample" dumped into a router and sent to try to find a survey I could qualify for.

The data exists—use it

When George Gallup sent out interviewers to find random households, the world was a different place. People were known, perhaps, to their neighbors. But they were not knowable en masse.

Today, there is information on us everywhere. Every credit card transaction, every click online, everywhere we go with our smartphone in tow leaves a data trail. That's why the same ad for dog food follows you around the internet for a week. That's why a search for a vacation place finds you inundated with helpful suggestions from destinations like those you searched. People are knowable.

Steve Cierpicki of Virgin Australia notes that, with the digitization of life, we expect transactions to be easier, and we assume information about us is known: "One big trend we've noticed is transacting generally. In the old days you might actually have to take your bill down to the post office to pay it with a cheque. You had to write the cheque, go down the post office, join the queue, just to pay for your electricity or your gas. Even with money, you'd have to have the currency, and then you'd pay for your purchase and then they'd give you the change, and you'd count it out, and you'd put it in your pocket...minutes of effort. And now, in Australia, we've got payWave. And you buy stuff just by tapping your card on a counter."

"We really notice that difference in transactions between the old-world businesses and the new-world businesses. So, some of the new-world businesses that we are dealing with, if you want to purchase something, literally all the information is there. You click on the e-mail, and wow, 'They already know all that?' Great. Instant. It's done."

"I think with surveys, it's the same thing," Cierpicki says. "Why would you get people to fill out forms when that information exists somewhere?"

His colleague Jade Buckler adds, "As a customer-led business, you shouldn't have to ask them if they're a frequent flyer and what tier they are. You should already know that they went in the lounge, and ask them questions about the lounge."

Wilding-Brown also suggests we need to get past this profiling problem and shorten surveys. She feels we can do this if we use data more intelligently. "That data exists on me: you just have to go and find it, right? And not be so myopic in the way that you look at data. You must look beyond the self-reported session. There's a lot of data about me, but garnering it is going to require you to be innovative, and dependent on third-party sources, and then to bundle it together to create a fuller picture of who I am as a consumer," she says. "You just have to get smarter on how to get it from me, and stop being so lazy."

Peter Harris suggests harnessing this existing data trail allows "brands to talk to the people that they want and to know a lot more about them without having to ask them all the questions again, enabling respondents to really provide some of that nuanced information to help us really understand the why." The vision that Harris and Wilding-Brown describe is vastly better than being disqualified over and over again.

We need to show respect for people by putting the pieces of the puzzle together. We need to care enough to set our interactions up for success. Creating communities where you can combine survey data with profiling information and—crucially—customer data allows you to sidestep many of these disqualification problems almost entirely and give people the kind of experience they expect.

Stop asking questions people struggle to answer

Ray Poynter of #NewMR makes the point that while length is a problem, there are more profound difficulties in how we ask questions. "The most obvious way that surveys are abusive is their length; we hear of 30- and even 40-minute surveys," Poynter says. "But we can dig a bit further and find a deeper problem: survey questions reflect the brand's perspective, not the customers' – which results in questions that lack relevance to the research participants."

"A brand may be interested in the ten leading products in a market," Poynter points out, "but the participant might only be interested in the two brands he or she likes, along with a clear view of two brands that he or she strongly dislikes. The brand may want participants to scale their views on a 0 to 10 scale, but writers such as Stanislas Dehaene have shown us that people do not use numbers in that way." We need to stop putting the brand's needs first. It doesn't work.

Here is a typical market research question; "Thinking of the last ten times you purchased a chocolate/candy bar, which of the following brands did you purchase? (If you purchased a brand not on this list please write in the name of the brand in 'other.')"

What are the odds you remember the last 10 times you bought a candy bar? For me, I'd guess that would go back about 3 or 4 years. And do I remember what I bought? No. But I can guess, and if you ask me to, I will. I am just not sure how good that information will be.

"Please rate brand X on how well it meets your nutritional needs, using a scale of 1 to 5 where 5 is very closely associated and 1 is not closely associated at all."

What are my "nutritional needs"? Do I know? Do I ever think about that? And what's with the 1 to 5 scale? When was the last time someone said, "Hey, how's it going?" and you brightly replied "4"! If we treat our respondents as people, we won't ask questions they can't answer.

Annie Pettit has written a valuable and very readable book about writing surveys—a handbook that recognizes that respondents are people. The title of the book, *People Aren't Robots: A practical guide to the psychology and technique of questionnaire design*, speaks volumes. In an email exchange, I asked her about her thoughts on the way surveys are written today. She marveled at how we can expect things of "sample" that we can't do ourselves.

"We forget what we've bought, we misremember where we've shopped, and we rationalize that we buy things because we need them, not because we want them. But when it comes time to communicate with people participating in our research, we instantly block out our own illogical behaviors, and expect them to remember precise SKUs, stores, dates and times, and so many other meticulous details about every purchase decision they've ever made. That is the definition of illogical."

"We expect people to not get tired, bored, forgetful, or distracted when participating in research about topics that are only interesting to the brand manager," Pettit continued. "We expect people answering questionnaires to choose valid answers when none of the answer options apply to them, and provide diverse responses to grid questions that demand straight-lining. And rather than getting annoyed at our own failure to plan for and design research that accounts for the illogical creature that is the human being, we instead call people liars, cheaters, and fraudsters. Market researchers are supposed to understand and be empathetic towards the illogical, forgetful, perfectly imperfect human being."

People are not robots, they are people. Our questions need to put their needs, limitations and desires first, if we want good information.

Start putting people first

Mendy Orimland suggests we need to adopt a "respondent-first" approach to designing research. That's a deceptively simple phrase, with immense implications. A respondent-first approach involves doing what Pettit and Poynter suggest: not asking questions people struggle to answer. It also includes short surveys with a clear strategic objective. It avoids hiding behind mirrors and pretending we are not human too. It necessitates profiling and bringing in other streams of information, so that we don't ask irrelevant questions, and we don't invite people to participate in a survey—only to push them away when they don't own a turtle.

"If you have a respondent-first approach," Orimland says, "you will have happy respondents, happy data, happy researchers, and happy insights."

A people-first approach also involves giving back.

Give the people what they want

The people who answer our surveys are generous with their time, and often patient with our obscure and difficult-to-answer questions. The question is why? Why are they giving us their time and energy when there are so many competing demands for people's time? Do they do it for the money?

In a word, no. Professor Anja Göritz, a psychologist at the University of Freiburg in Germany, conducted a meta-analysis of the effectiveness of incentives and wrote about it in *Incentives in Web Studies: Methodological Issues and a Review.*

Her analysis revealed that "material incentives increase response and decrease drop-out," but "the combined effect of incentives on response and retention is still small." She found that incentives generally increased the response rate about 5% over what it would have been otherwise.

Göritz also reminds readers that "using material incentives is only one option to influence data quality and quantity. We should not forget about other possibly response-enhancing techniques such as personalization, pre-notification, deadlines, reminders, the offering of result summaries, and altruistic appeal."

Knowing how important intrinsic motivation is, and how unimportant money is, we tried an experiment: across a large sample of general population omnibus surveys in the U.S., UK and Canada, we cut the incentive for respondents in half. The response rate went from an average of 30% at the higher incentive to 31% at the lower amount. And these omnibus surveys are representative of the population.

The Angus Reid Institute, a research-focused charitable foundation, used these omnibuses to do election polling. According to Nate Silver's 538.com website, those election polls caused the foundation to be ranked as the most accurate of all the online survey samples they include in their comprehensive "pollster" ratings. And by the Angus Reid Institute's account, they correctly predicted 95% of recent national, state and provincial elections in the U.S. and Canada, using these Maru/Blue market communities.

It seems clear, from our experience, that representative samples of the public are not doing these surveys simply for the money.

"We've got to stop paying people for their information," Amirahmadi says. "Rather, we've got to try and find ways to create value for them to be involved." To create value, we need to understand why people do surveys.

What they like about doing research

Research suggests people answer our surveys because they want to have their voice heard. They want to contribute to society. They want to shape the future. And they want to learn.

We asked some people, in a video interview, what three things they would tell a friend they liked about doing surveys. One gentleman said, "Being chosen: that makes you feel as though you have a worthy opinion. The second thing would be to take part and give your opinion, speak on what it is you feel strongly about, and feel like you're contributing something, and at the same time learning something."

An older woman suggested, "I like giving my comments, and I like giving my opinions. I become more informed and I like to review the products as well." A young man's three things were "coming up with opinions about stuff I don't usually think of, being exposed to new marketing ideas, and learning about new companies." Another person suggested, "The best thing about doing surveys is you're able to influence others' opinions. You know your answer will be taken into consideration for future products. It's important that companies recognize your opinion because essentially, by doing surveys, you are shaping the world around you."

Being a researcher, I wanted to quantify these ideas, to see if they mattered to most people. We found these sentiments to be very prevalent. Roughly 9 in 10 agreed:

"I feel like I am being a trusted advisor when I provide feedback to a company on their products."

"I feel like I am doing my part as a good consumer and citizen when I provide feedback," and "Doing surveys is one way I can contribute to society."

"I do surveys because I want organizations to know where I stand on issues."

"I enjoy learning about new things and products when I do surveys."

"I feel like my opinion makes a difference."

These are the kinds of beliefs that build a better society. These are people who contribute, and hope that their efforts are being respected and understood. We need to honor that.

Christy Ransom is a person who wakes up every day thinking about how to engage the people who join an insight community. She is the VP of Engagement Strategy at Vision Critical and has been working on how to engage people for the past 10 years.

She says it is important to start by thinking about why people join. "People join an insight community for many of the same reasons they might join a book club or any group with a common interest: they want to feel that they belong to something special and unique, that they are contributing to a greater good, that their involvement has influence on decisions, and that they have a sense of connection to other members in the same community. To build and maintain engagement with people in online communities, you simply appeal to those needs and members will respond." She suggests it is also important to "Do a pulse check now and then to see if members feel like they are getting what they expected out of the community experience and adjust accordingly."

Making a difference

"People like to know that their input meant something and it's going to make a difference," says Michael Haynes, consultant and author of *Listen Innovate Grow*. "At least it's been recognized, and it's been recognized by people who matter." Showing people their opinion is recognized involves providing feedback to them and dropping the cloak of anonymity. That's something researchers have typically been loath to do (hence the charade of hiding behind mirrors). They are rightly concerned that knowing who is behind the question could change the answer. That can be a problem, in a few circumstances. But in other situations, it is a huge plus.

Shawn Henry runs several communities that are sponsored by specific companies and are branded as such. He finds branding the community encourages more engaged participation when people know their voice is being heard and their point of view considered. "They basically signed up because they are actually interested in the industry, interested in the company, and they want to see the company do better stuff," he says. "So, from a respondent point of view, a branded community is much more engaged in the sense that they are quite interested in the topic, or they are quite interested in the company, and they will actually want to get better service from the company. So, they are happy to provide that feedback."

Harris echoes that idea. He finds that people respond better if they have an interest in the outcome. "It's been proven that if you can get people into a community environment they're not likely to be more positive or extremely negative about you," he suggests. "They just want to help the brand. So, they give you a more balanced view. On the Telstra community now, after eight or nine years, we find people that are better at critiquing ideas and will really get into the detail, what needs to happen, because they feel like they have a vested interest." Henry adds, "it's less about some vague reward, much more about 'I'm appreciating you asking me this question to actually change stuff.'"

"I think stepping through the mirror and revealing who you are is that first stage of getting somebody else to open up," Amirahmadi says. "Here's my name. What's yours?" He has learned from experience that revealing the name of the sponsor can have positive effects: "We were launching our Prudential community; that was the first insurance community that we launched in Asia. And we were quite concerned that people would never want to talk about insurance. Like, who's going to want to join an insurance community? And it's one of the best-responding, longest-term communities that we've got. Because if you genuinely show that you're listening, and you're interested, then people will talk, even about insurance."

Making a personal connection is also something Ransom finds is important. She suggests that, as a person managing a community, it is good to "introduce yourself with your picture and everything. It generates more of a connection with people, and they feel more like they're talking to you one-on-one instead of it being, 'Oh, I'm just sending this to this large company.' I don't think it is as impactful as, 'Hey, I'm just sitting here wanting to know what you think about this.' Even though it's going out to 3,000 people or whatever, people don't feel that way; they feel like it's personalized. And it makes a big difference."

It is also important that people are clear about the purpose of the community and what kind of impact they might have. Ransom told me about a "sports company that had a community that was based on being a fan, which implied there would be activities focused on the sport, rules and players." People joined because they were excited about having an influence on the sport. But the reality was the community was "really for the brand's ad partners." The questions were not about the sport, but about what people bought. Because of the disconnect between expectations and reality "engagement dropped considerably," she said.

But when they "re-launched the community with a more honest approach to the intent of the community: 'We want to understand more about you, our fans.'" As a result, she says, "People weren't bothered by the survey asking what laundry soap they use. It was a matter of setting expectations and delivering."

This sense of the importance of being listened to reflects the sentiment of the respondent we cited earlier who said, "by doing surveys, you are shaping the world around you." Amirahmadi tells a story: "I was with a client today at Kellogg's, and he was trying to understand the concept of value exchange between the customer and the brand. And I said, 'Well, look, have you ever launched a product or an ad?' And he said, 'Yeah, I've launched many products and ads over the years.' I said, 'Okay, whenever you walk through the supermarket, or when you have been watching the TV with a partner, or a friend, or a mother, or father, or child or whatever, have you said to them' 'Oh, I helped create that product,' or, 'I helped create that ad'?' I think we've all done that."

"And you feel good about it, right? It gives you a feeling of, 'I'm a bit special; I've got some kudos. There's something in the real world that I helped create.' All our clients feel that emotion. If you take that emotion that the client is feeling and then bottle it up, you can feed it to your community members to make them feel like, 'Wow, I actually helped create that; I feel good about the things that I've done. That further engages me and makes me want to be involved in the future.' It's a combination of showing you listen, and then acknowledging that they've played a role in changing things."

Outside of an ongoing community, we have found that people respond well to in-survey feedback. My colleague Kim Arnold and her team did a study which included one small set of questions for the purpose of engaging respondents and providing feedback. At the end of a survey on artificial intelligence (AI), they included some fun "fact or fiction" questions about AI. Then they showed people their score on the test, and some brief additional information on AI. At the end of the survey, they asked some standard questions about how interesting the survey was, and how much they enjoyed it.

They then compared the interest and enjoyment results from that study to a set of 16 other similar studies done with the same population. This feedback mechanism increased levels of interest and enjoyment—and those levels were high to begin with.

Feedback like that is a simple thing, but it sends a signal to people that their opinion is heard and valued. An even simpler feedback mechanism is, at the end of a survey, to show people how they answered some sort of opinion statement and how other respondents answered too. It can be as simple as "earlier you said you agreed strongly that 'things are changing too fast these days.' Here's how other people answered." It's an easy exercise that can be incorporated into any survey, and people enjoy it.

Letting people know their voice is heard is about building relations. It's one aspect of treating respondents like people.

Where next?

We need to stop writing long surveys, and start crafting short ones we'd invite our friends and family to answer. We must stop looking at interviews from a researcher's perspective, and start viewing them through the eyes of the people who are answering. We need to stop disqualifying people, and start profiling them.

We also need to stop just taking people's information, and start giving feedback that lets people know their contribution is important. There is significant value to our industry in telling people how they are making a difference. Sharing information on decisions made, products changed, and insights generated can help people understand their effort is worthwhile.

We've heard the voice of the people. We depend on them for our livelihood. We know what they like. Let's give them the survey experience they deserve. Let's treat them like people.

Chapter 8 – Stop Asking Complicated Questions and Start Asking Questions People Can Answer

Researchers get attached to the way they ask questions. There is also significant pressure to maintain a consistent approach because it allows for prior study comparisons and the development of normative databases. For companies like Nielsen's BASES, who do forecasting, or Kantar Millward Brown, who do ad testing and tracking, normative databases are the foundations upon which their businesses are built.

Changing the way questions are asked upends all of that, and threatens the valuation of large chunks of the industry. But the reality is we must change, radically.

Long grids? Soon to be in the dustbin of history. Complex scales? Farewell. Thinking about adopting mobile first design? Too late, the world is already moving on. Why? Because the way people communicate is changing and fragmenting.

I email my father-in-law but text my children. My kids Snapchat with their friends. I might ask Siri to tell me the weather. Or maybe I will type "what is the forecast?" People choose multiple methods of communication depending on where they are and with whom they are interacting. As researchers, we have no choice but to adapt to these fragmenting and fluid modes of communication. If we don't adapt, we will become irrelevant, because our data will not be representative.

A matter of life and death

A paper presented at a recent ESOMAR Big Data conference underscored just how important it is to communicate with people using the method they want. For this study, having the best data available was literally a matter of life and death.

The presentation described a public health study focused on combating the Zika virus in Brazil. The study collected answers to questions, as well as geolocation data and photographs. Concerns about Zika have faded today, but at the time of the 2016 Olympic Games in Rio, there were questions about whether the Games should be cancelled or postponed—because of the danger of spreading the disease. The Zika virus was ravaging large portions of Brazil. Stopping Zika was critical. This study helped control the disease.

A very large sample was needed because the data was being used to map areas where there were breeding grounds for mosquitoes. The more data they could get, and the more representative the data was, the more effectively they could allocate public health resources.

This was a high-stakes effort, where getting rich representative data was not an academic exercise. It was the difference between eradicating Zika or allowing it to spread and ravage the population. That's why they connected with people using multiple methods.

The Brazilian researchers surveyed 300,000 people through email. They also connected with 400,000 through text invites. But those numbers together were less than the 750,000 people they contacted through WhatsApp, an app common in Brazil.

The research identified areas where there was standing water near where people lived. By surveying over a million people they generated maps that guided the health department in eradicating breeding grounds for mosquitos. As a result, they largely halted the spread of Zika.

Imagine if they had only used email to survey people. How well would that have worked? What would the geographic biases have been? How many more people would have contracted the virus because of the misses?

The Zika study shows us the importance of connecting with people through the communication mediums they want, but its lessons do not address a much larger issue looming on the horizon: the way we communicate is morphing. Right now, many people are moving away from text and toward voice.

When Siri asks the questions

It is anticipated that three quarters of all U.S. households will have a voice-activated virtual assistant like an Amazon Alexa or Google Home by 2021. Current estimates suggest the market for voice-activated virtual assistants will be about $16 billion by 2020, five times larger than it was in 2017. Alexa, Siri, and their friends will soon impact many, many things—including research.

Changing from text to voice is not just another switch of the medium. It can also alter how we act and what we expect. Antonio Garcia Martinez, writing in *Wired*, describes a recent epiphany he had: "I spent an afternoon in a quasi *Her*-style romance with my Amazon Echo, shopping for items, organizing my calendar, messaging friends, and rather less usefully, trying to get Alexa to say something obscene or witty (and only partially succeeding). Fast forward four hours later. I'm in my car, when one of those things I forgot to either buy or search for on Amazon pops into my head."

"'Alexa!' I imperiously shouted into the empty interior of my car, ready to have the global brain do my bidding. The wave of felt stupidity and embarrassment that hit me after was almost as strong as the realization that something had just snapped in my relationship with computing."

"Using a keyboard and mouse to manipulate a computer after successfully using voice feels about the same as using a command-line interface on an old UNIX machine after using a graphical interface."

His prediction: "Between touchscreens and voice, most people in the future won't even know how to touch-type, and typing will go back to being a specialist practitioner's skill, limited to long-form authors, programmers, and (perhaps) antiquarian hipsters who also own fixies and roast their own coffee. My 2-year-old daughter will likely never learn how to drive…instead issuing voice commands to her self-driving car. And she'll also not know what QWERTY is, or have her left pinkie wired to the mental notion of the letter "Q," as I do so subconsciously I reach for it without even thinking. Instead, she'll speak into an empty room and expect the global hive-mind, along with its AI handmaidens, to answer."

Whether Martinez's vision of a "global hive-mind" with "AI handmaidens" comes to pass remains to be seen. However, people who embrace voice assistants are unlikely to sit down at a desktop and answer a survey with long grids and complex scales. And they are not going to be interested in waiting while Alexa reads out 12 answer options and then asks how they should be rank ordered. They won't see the lists and they certainly won't recall—let alone be able to rank order—all 12 options.

The way we ask questions will have to change.

Most millennials in North America are already interested in doing surveys using virtual assistants, according to our research. We expect that number to increase dramatically. That means we need to move quickly to embrace device-agnostic ways of asking questions.

We require methods of gathering information that will work on virtual assistants, mobile devices, computers and whatever new technology emerges. This will compel us to move away from long questions, complex scales, and grids, and force us toward simpler questions.

Last century methods meet a new world

When survey research began, its approach to measurement was heavily influenced by the psychometrics of the day. Psychometricians' concern was obtaining the most precise measurement possible, in the form of scales to measure things like illnesses and IQ. They designed questionnaires with the idea they would be administered by carefully trained interviewers, and were less concerned with convenience and lack of attentiveness on the part of the person answering the questionnaire. That was fine when surveys were administered in a face-to-face environment, by an interviewer, but those are not the conditions under which people do surveys today.

The types of questions and scales used in market research have changed very little since the last century. It's time to move on.

The upside of change

Questions like "yes or no" and "hot or not" are simple enough that it does not matter whether you are on a tablet or talking to Siri. They are a lot quicker and easier to answer. That's part of the upside of abandoning some of the old methods.

Our research has shown that binary questions are 2 to 3 times faster to answer than scaled questions. That's because scales are taxing to answer. It didn't matter to psychometricians in the 1900's, who were seeking absolute precision, that a person had to concentrate to answer their questions. It was the interviewer's job to keep them engaged. But in our multi-tasking, attention-fractured world, we don't have that luxury.

Scales are hard and slow for people to answer because of the way our brains are wired. When people look at (or listen to) a scale, they must perceive the number of points, make a judgment as to which number or word represents their feeling, and then find the spot on the scale where that word or number is. Sounds simple enough.

But people have a hard time accurately distinguishing between items when quantities increase. We are good with one, two or three items. Then it gets harder. We are either forced to pay more attention, or we tend to make mistakes. Often, even when we pay more attention, we still make errors.

"The fact that there is a strict limit on the number of objects that we are able to enumerate at once has been known to psychologists for more than a century," reports French cognitive neuroscientist Stanislas Dehaene. "In 1886, James McKeen Cattell, in his laboratory in Leipzig, demonstrated that when subjects were briefly shown a card bearing several black dots, they could enumerate them with unfailing precision only if their number did not exceed three. Beyond this limit errors accumulated." At the same time as errors grow, the time taken to respond slows down, once you get past counting three things. After four, the number of errors and the amount of time required to process the numbers increase at a linear rate.

So, the upside of being forced away from complex scales is that surveys become quicker and easier for people. But we can't give up the added precision that comes from scales, can we?

Sensitivity of scales

The idea behind a scale is that it takes a more nuanced measurement that should lead you to a better insight or decision. We tested that idea in a series of studies in which we compared binary measures (like "I'd buy it" or "hot or not") to commonly used scales like the likelihood of purchase, 5-point brand association measures and the 11-point Net Promoter Score. We found that, in almost every case, the binary measures were as closely, or more closely, correlated with spend or purchase behavior. In other tests, we found that binary measures were more sensitive than traditional scales in differentiating between winning and losing messages and product concepts. We're not the first researchers to find that binary questions work well.

An international group of psychometricians and physicians created a binary version of a commonly used health questionnaire, because they wanted something that was faster and easier for patients to answer. They concluded, in the careful language of medical journal articles, that "Overall, the testing comparison produces results indicating that the binary recoding of the SF-36 scales meets at least similar standards without jeopardizing the underlying structure of the original format" and "our results indicate that the SF-36 binary recoding gives the possibility to suggest a new version of smarter and easier methodology of administration . . . ."

Another group of academics was more direct. "Quick, simple and reliable: forced binary survey questions" is the title of their paper. Their abstract wraps up the whole issue so succinctly it is worth a read:

"Consumers are increasingly saturated by market research, which leads to decreasing response rates and an increased danger of response bias. Market researchers thus face the challenge of recruiting respondents, increasing response rates and reducing respondent fatigue by making questionnaires as short and pleasant as possible. One way of achieving this is to replace traditionally used ordinal multi-category answer formats (such as Likert scales) with forced binary scales. This proposition is only attractive if it indeed shortens the survey time while not compromising the quality of managerial insights from the data."

"This study investigates these conditions. Results from a repeat-measurement design indicate that managerial interpretations do not differ substantially between the two answer formats, responses are equally reliable, and that the binary format is quicker and perceived as less complex."

While we might be reluctant to change the kinds of questions we ask, we should take heart that newer, simpler types of questions will gather equivalent data, more quickly, and with happier respondents.

But change is hard

While there is an upside to change, it will be difficult. Minsk says, "I think the industry is at a crossroads right now, similar in some ways to what we went through 20 years ago with the transition from paper to phone, and in person to online. Some of those challenges are going to be the same, as far as establishing validity. But I think it's very different in other ways, in that 20 years ago we were moving from one tool to another tool, and it was a very discrete cut-off."

The coming changes have far-reaching implications, Minsk suggests. "The goal becomes asking questions in the right way, for the right consumer, in the right context, on the right device. It is also what can you not ask, what can you observe, what can you append from other existing data."

This is not a trivial change, and it will be difficult to convince people to accept change, he suggests. "Never underestimate the power of 'that's how we've always done it,' even among really, really smart people," he cautions.

People think "the way we've always done it" is the better way, and the longer it has been done that way, the better it seems to be. It's an unconscious bias.

Psychologist Scott Eidelman and his colleagues did a series of studies in which two groups of people were shown the same thing. Some were told it was newer. Others were informed it was older. For example, they had people taste a root beer. Some were told it has been made that way since 1903. Other were instructed it had been made since 2003. Guess which one tasted better?

In every case, whether it was acupuncture, enhanced interrogations, degree requirements or soft drinks, "the longer it was said to exist, the better it was evaluated." We have an unconscious bias toward the status quo. It is a bias we must acknowledge.

There is also a fear of abandoning tried and true methods. "If change feels like walking off a cliff blindfolded, then people will reject it.

People will often prefer to remain mired in misery than to head toward an unknown," wrote Rosabeth Moss Kanter in *Harvard Business Review*. "As the saying goes, 'Better the devil you know than the devil you don't know.'"

As Minsk explains, "I have 20 years of built-up benchmarks, and I know how to get in front of senior management and present a BASES study and talk about Top Two Box. If I have to transition to an entirely different approach to validate concepts, how do I do that? How do I make comparisons? How do I make decisions?"

"I think it's going to take people on the client side recognizing that, 'You know what? A five-point purchase interest scale in context of a monadic concept test may not be producing the results that I think it's producing.' One thing that may push people is some spectacular failures of validation," Minsk suggests. "I think that if we continue with our current approaches we're going to see our research results diverge from what we see in market."

That concern about the unknown, about being sure about what you are measuring, is why we did research comparing things like binary versions of a concept test with the classic measures championed by Nielsen's BASES. We published it, and other studies like it, because we feel it's important that we all learn, and develop greater comfort in embracing new ways.

There will need to be a great deal of research on research in our collective future. We'll be required to prove we're getting the same answers on different devices. We must demonstrate that we would make the same or better strategic decisions based on new ways of working. And we can't afford to wait until we start experiencing the "spectacular failures" Minsk mentions.

With the pace of technological change today, it is probable new forms of connecting and communicating will sprout up like mushrooms overnight. We won't have the luxury of adapting to them slowly.

Companies with large databases of normative data are particularly troubled by change. They have a huge amount of equity in those databases—equity they can't afford to give up on. But the reality is, they can either choose to change their ways and accept that their normative data will not be 100% comparable, or they can double down on the status quo, and then slowly but surely watch the value of their investment evaporate.

Change in the value of normative data is inevitable, either by choice or by default.

The "Chobani incident"

The necessity of embracing new ways of collecting information was driven home by a story told to me by Lisa Wilding-Brown, Chief Research Officer of Innovate MR. Back in the early 2010s, she was working with a research company that was focused on embracing mobile devices in research. She was brought in to help a food manufacturer completely retool their research program in a more mobile-friendly way. They were revamping their approach because this company had learned the cost of not embracing change the hard way.

They suffered what she called "a war-wound of epic proportions." It involved the "Chobani incident."

The company had a very popular yogurt that was a dominant brand in the category. "It was a strong brand for many, many years," she explained. "They were innovating with many different flavors—very unique flavors. They thought 'we pretty much have this market cornered.' And, before they knew it, Greek yogurt, as a new trend, sort of crept up on them. None of the data they had been collecting, month over month, year over year, had pointed to this trend that was emerging. Greek yogurt stole a huge share of the market, and the entire insights team was wiped out as a result."

"They were completely reliant on the traditional methods of data collection. They were doing online quant, longitudinal work, year over year, and had made no changes to the survey instrument, and completely excluded the role that mobile had in the space."

"Millennials and Gen Z are huge users of mobile. That's their go-to. They are very mobile-centric in the way that they operate as consumers, and mobile was excluded as a research methodology for the food manufacturer. They were just doing basic online quant via desktop. So, they were excluding a huge portion of the population and ultimately the voice of the customer." As a result, they "completely gutted the insights group" and "let the whole team go."

Sounds like a fate we'd all like to avoid.

Change comes faster and faster

The faster you drive, the further ahead you must look. The rate of technological change is accelerating rapidly and will continue to alter how we communicate. We need to vigilantly peer into the distance, ready to change the questions we ask.

The questions that survive these turbulent times will have to be simple, quick, and easy to answer on any device. There will be an inevitable period of uncomfortable change. But that's better than a "Chobani incident."

What's Next?

"What would research look like today if it was just starting from scratch? How would the Silicon Valley of research prioritize their investments?"
Katrina Galas, sports marketer

For years, Netflix asked people to rate the content they watched with a 5-star rating system, so that Netflix could make more accurate recommendations about what people would want to watch. A little while ago they ditched that in favor of a simpler thumbs up or thumbs down rating because, according to *Variety*, the "thumbs-based ratings deliver more accurate recommendations and they're easier for people to understand than the five-star scale. The company said that in testing, it saw a 200% increase in ratings by users with the thumbs-up/thumbs-down system." Now they have dropped customer ratings altogether, presumably because behavioral models were better predictors of choice.

Does Netflix's approach to ratings foreshadow the future of the insights industry? A move from scales, to binary, to behavior? Perhaps.

The story of Netflix's rating system points us to the need to think past methodology to action. I don't think we'll see the end of the survey any time soon, but I do think it will become just one tool among many that the insights professional must wield with considerable self-confidence. We need to be laser-focused on what Haynes boiled down to "So what? What's next?", and not be distracted by where the information comes from.

Sauriol summed up the sentiment of a lot of insights professionals when he told me, "Of all my favorite projects, the ones I'm most proud of, and those that have had the most impact, are projects where we had that approach of working together, toward an action. Whereas the ones that are a drain were more traditional and transactional. I hope as an organization we keep pushing for an integrated approach because it makes it more fun, honestly." Spoken like a true insights professional. Taking action is much more fun than taking orders.

Greco is bullish about the future: "I feel optimistic for research because I think there are more questions than ever before. As a researcher, I think it's a really exciting time because there are so many paths and different directions to go. It's a good place for people who are innovative and smart and want to explore new worlds."

Harris is equally optimistic. "There has never been a better time to be in the industry and profession if you're willing to change, step up and take action. It is much scarier being directly responsible for the customer than simply doing projects on the topic. But it's much more exciting."

Minsk is also enthusiastic about the possibilities, but he knows that the journey will not be without its discomforting challenges. "I think insights groups that are driven by making an impact on their business, by being a thought leader and a thought challenger, will be able to put the consumer front and center. I can see how the insights industry and client-side researchers are on the verge of a golden age of being able to insert the consumer into decision-making in a way that we've never been able to do before."

He says, "It's going to take will, and discipline, and courage for us to change the way that we do things, to bring our marketing partners along, and to really think hard about what we do. We need to make some tough decisions and some tough changes. But it will be worth it."

It will be worth it indeed. Bon voyage!

Acknowledgements

First, and foremost, I'd like to thank the researchers, marketers and strategists who shared their thoughts about the future of the insights industry. As you have seen from the copious quotes, they had many brilliant things to say. Thanks to all of you for sharing your time and knowledge with me and everyone reading this book. The interviews were a delight, and tremendously enriching.

The kind people who offered us their wisdom are, in alphabetical order: Maz Amirahmadi; Antony Barton; Jila Bick; Jade Buckler; Steven Cierpicki; Patrick Comer; Reg Downs; Ihno Froehling; Katrina Galas; Anamaria Gotelli; Michael Greco; Elias Hadaya; Peter Harris; Michael Haynes; Shawn Henry; Paul Holtzman; Eleonora Jonusiene; Maggie Kishibe; Shigeru Kishikawa; Seth Minsk; Pamela Mittoo; Elizabeth Moore; Jaideep Mukerji; Meghan Nameth; Mendy Orimland; Annie Pettit; Ray Poynter; Finn Raben; Christy Ransom; Kristopher Sauriol; Pina Sciarra; Howard Shimmel; Mike Stevens; Vidya Subramani and Lisa Wilding-Brown.

If you are reading this far, you are probably a researcher with an interest in the details. You might wonder about how these people were selected. They are not a random, representative sample. They are a convenience sample, collected using a snowball method. Thank you to friends, colleagues and all those who made introductions.

Having been at the insights game for over 30 years, there are too many colleagues to thank by name. People from the Angus Reid Group, Ipsos-Reid, Ipsos Health, Angus Reid Strategies, Vision Critical and Maru/Matchbox have all taught me much, and shaped my views more than I know.

There are a few people who, through sheer longevity of association, need to be called out. Teresa Lam, Vice President of Data Services at Maru/Matchbox has put up with me for 28 years—and through all of them she has been unfailingly efficient, accurate and brutally honest. I have been learning from Jane Tang, head of the Advanced Analytics team, for 24 enriching years. Ed Morawski, former COO of Maru/Matchbox, and I had lots of adventures together over 21 good years. I must also thank Dr. Angus Reid, who let me take the ball and run with it, right from the very beginning. Thank you for all the opportunities.

Megan Paul has been the front line in-house editor for this book, and all the Maru/Matchbox articles and whitepapers we produce. She asks great questions, notices a million things that I have missed and is never afraid to share her opinion. Many thanks, for everything.

Michael Cusden, our social media expert, has been gently coaching me—a social mediaphobe—in how to amplify the messages of this book. Thank you for your patience and support.

Grant Heckman is an exceptional writer, teacher and editor. I was greatly encouraged when he agreed to come on board as editor, because I have a great deal of respect for his work (and his musicianship). His encouragement, love of language, excellent suggestions and attention to detail enriched this book immensely.

Any remaining mistakes you see in this book are mine. Such is life.

A big thank you to my wife, Yola Zdanowicz. She's an amazing research methodologist, strategist and storyteller, whose perspective on insights has been influencing my own for almost 20 years. Thanks also to the lads: Cameron, Colin and Ian, who have lived through countless dinner table discussions about research, with relatively little eye rolling.

Finally, special thanks to Ged Parton, CEO of the Maru Group, for encouraging me to write this book. At the beginning of 2018, he said "write a book." So, I did.

References

Chapter 1

Rates of Dinosaur Body Mass Evolution Indicate 170 Million Years of Sustained Ecological Innovation on the Avian Stem Lineage, by Roger B. J. Benson, Nicolás E. Campione, Matthew T. Carrano, Philip D. Mannion, Corwin Sullivan, Paul Upchurch, David C. Evans. *PLOS biology.org*. May 6, 2014.

Bob Iger on the new storytelling, by Bob Iger. *The Economist. The World in 2018*. December 2017.

Mental Tests and Measurements by James McKeen Cattell, *Mind*. Volume 15. 1890.

"Survey Research in the United States: Roots and Emergence 1890-1960" by Jean M. Converse. Taylor and Francis, London and New York. 2009.

Mainstreet acknowledges 'catastrophic failure' in projections for Calgary mayoral race, by Reid Southwick, *calgaryherald.com*. October 17, 2017.

Statement on Calgary Municipal Election Polling by Quito Maggi. *mainstreetresearch.ca*. October 19, 2017.

Mainstreet Research rescinds letter threatening legal action against Nenshi's campaign pollster by Brooks DeCillia. *cbc.ca*. Dec 11, 2017.

How Data Failed Us in Calling an Election by Steve Lohr and Natasha Singer. *nytimes.com*. November 10, 2016.

The Politics of Polling by the House of Lords Select Committee on Political Polling and Digital Media. *publications.parliament.uk*. April 17, 2018.

"Wonky" Calgary election polling under investigation, by Trish Audette-Longo. *nationalobserver.com* October 26th, 2017.

Three eras of survey research by Robert M. Groves. *The Public Opinion Quarterly, Volume 75, Number 5*. December 1, 2011.

Chapter 2

Building an Insights Engine by Frank van den Driest, Stan Sthanunathan and Keith Weed. *Harvard Business Review*. September 2016.

Market Research Knowledge Benchmarking Study 2018 by Ray Poynter and Sue York. *newmr.org*. August 2018

Re-imagining the client-side insight function by Andrew Geoghegan. *ESOMAR Congress*. September 2017.

Chapter 3

"The thinking of thoughts" by Gilbert Ryle. University of Saskatchewan. 1968.

"The Invisible Gorilla: How Our Intuitions Deceive Us" by Christopher Chabris and Daniel Simons. Random House. New York. 2009. You can see the video at theinvisiblegorilla.com.

The fallacy of obviousness by Teppo Felin. *aeon.co*. July 5, 2018.

It takes many notes to make a symphony: The power of data cross pollination by Ritanbara Mundrey. *ESOMAR Congress*. September 2017.

Chapter 4

"Stumbling on Happiness" by Dan Gilbert. Random House of Canada. Toronto. 2007.

"Thinking, fast and slow" by Daniel Kahneman. Farrar, Strauss and Giroux. New York. 2011.

"The Mind is Flat: The Illusion of Mental Depth and The Improvised Mind" by Nick Chater. Allen Lane. London. 2018.

"Why: what happens when people give reasons...and why" by Charles Tilly. Princeton University Press. 2008.

Chapter 5

John Day letter to the Lord Grand Admiral, Winter 1497/8, The Smugglers' City, Dept. of History, University of Bristol.

(Still) Boringly Reliable: Evidence of the Consistency of Maru/Blue Market Community Sample by Andrew Grenville and Rob Berger. *Marublue.net*. 2018.

Chapter 6

FiveThirtyEight's Pollster Ratings. fivethirtyeight.com

Horsemeat found in Ikea meatballs in Europe by The Associated Press. *cbc.ca*. Feb 25, 2013.

Art or Science? The Perils and Possibilities of Survey Sampling in the Evolving Online World by Andrew Grenville and Rob Berger. *Marumatchbox.com*. 2016.

Rivers, Routers and Reality – A Test of Sample Sources, Data Quality and Reliability by Andrew Grenville and Rob Berger. *Marumatchbox.com*. 2016.

Online Panel Research: A data quality perspective, edited by Mario Callegaro, Reg Baker, Jelke Bethlehem, Anja S. Goritz, Jon A. Krosnick & Paul J Lavarkas. Wiley. 2014

The High Cost of Cheap Sample: Evaluating the reliability and validity of a publisher- driven online sample source by Andrew Grenville and Rob Berger. *Marublue.net*. 2018.

Social Media Update 2016: Facebook usage and engagement is on the rise, while adoption of other platforms holds steady by Shannon Greenwood, Andrew Perrin and Maeve Duggan. *pewinternet.org*. November 11, 2016

Wine, Cheese, Scotch and Sample: Know the Source by Andrew Grenville and Rob Berger. *Marumatchbox.com*. 2017.

Last Call at the Sample Oasis: Sample sources and the impact on validity and reliability by Andrew Grenville and Rob Berger. *Marumatchbox.com*. 2016.

Incentives in Web Studies: Methodological Issues and a Review by Anja S. Goritz, *International Journal of Internet Science*. Volume 1. Number 1. 2006.

Judge online polling by real-world accuracy, not academic theory by Angus Reid. *angusreid.org.* 2018.

*Report on Focus Group Findings: ARF FOQ 2 Router Initia*tive by Steve Gittelman and Efrian Ribeiro. *Advertising Research Foundation.* 2012.

Chapter 7

Survey Respondents: The Polar Ice Caps of Market Research by Lisa Wilding-Brown Green. *GreenBook Blog.* February 22, 2016.

Effects of Questionnaire Length on Participation and Indicators of Response Quality in a Web Survey by Mirta Galesic and Michael Bosnjak. *Public Opinion Quarterly*, January 2009. Volume 73. Issue 2.

"People Aren't Robots: A practical guide to the psychology and technique of questionnaire design" by Annie Pettit. Available from Amazon. 2018.

Chapter 8

Big Data Bigger Impact: How data collection and updated technology can lead to great social impact by Maurício Maura. *ESOMAR Big Data World.* November 2017.

The Virtual Digital Assistant Market Will Reach $15.8 Billion Worldwide by 2021. Tractica.com. August 3, 2016.

The Veni, Vidi, Vici of Voice by Antonio García Martínez. *Wired.* February 20, 2018

The Future of Feedback: Consumer Interest in New Ways of Doing Research by Andrew Grenville. *Marumatchbox.com.* 2018.

"The Number Sense: How the mind creates mathematics" by Stanislas Dehaene. Oxford University Press. New York. 2011.

Changing Times Demand Rethinking Old Approaches: A case for quick reliable, easy to answer questions by Andrew Grenville, *Marumatchbox.com.* 2017.

Performance Comparison of Likert and Binary Formats of SF-36 Version 1.6 Across ECRHS II Adults Populations by Mario Grassi, PhD, Andrea Nucera, PhD, Elisabetta Zanolin, PhD, Ernst Omenaas, MD, Josep M. Anto, MD, Bénédicte Leynaert, PhD on behalf of the European Community Respiratory Health Study Quality of Life Working Group. *Value in Health.* Volume 10, Number 6, 2007.

Quick, simple and reliable: forced binary survey questions by S. Dolnicar, B. Grün, and F. Leisch. *International Journal of Market Research*, Volume 53, Number 2, 2011.

Bias in Favor of the Status Quo by Scott Eidelman and Christian S. Crandall. *Social and Personality Psychology Compass*, Volume 6, Number 3, 2012.

Ten Reasons People Resist Change by Rosabeth Moss Kanter. *Harvard Business Review.* September 25, 2012.

About Maru/Matchbox

Maru/Matchbox has been pushing the boundaries of the customer market insights space for over a decade. We are a sector-focused consumer intelligence firm focused entirely on better client outcomes. Our expert teams are deeply invested in key sectors of the economy, delivering insights and analysis backed by superior quality data.

For more information visit www.marumatchbox.com